Workforce Blueprint

A comprehensive resource for human resources (HR) professionals in technical industries, this book offers strategies and best practices for expanding and maintaining a diverse workforce, including company branding, community engagement/partnerships, training, and organizational culture considerations.

The pandemic and automation have forever changed how and where we work, what work we do, and who will do it. All this uncertainty has impacted talent pipelines in technical industries and highlighted the critical need for talent expansion and inclusion within this global sector. This book addresses the multifaceted challenges and opportunities that technical industries face in creating a diverse workforce, a unique context that has been overlooked in broader discussions of workplace diversity. It looks back on the history of diversity management and forward to best practices for expanding talent, including attracting, recruiting, and retaining all talent, including special populations. It provides a comprehensive understanding of the importance of inclusivity in manufacturing, construction, and engineering, along with tools and techniques for implementing these strategies in any organization. A Talent Expansion Framework is included to serve as a blueprint for improving the depth and breadth of talent through action-oriented approaches by leadership, the community, and employees themselves.

HR practitioners, business owners, and policymakers in technical industries and beyond will appreciate this book's focus on practical strategies and its actionable approach to acquiring, developing, and expanding talent.

Leressa Suber, PhD, PHR, SHRM-CP, has over 20 years of experience working at the intersection of business, education, and workforce within construction, manufacturing, and higher education. As a researcher and HR practitioner, her expertise strengthens leadership, HR performance, and diverse talent pipelines. As Principal at Bonsai Consulting Group, she consults with businesses, executives, and institutions to provide solutions to complex problems in HR management, training, workforce development, and program evaluation. Through coaching, facilitation, and real-world case studies, her work is transforming technical industries. She serves as an adjunct faculty member at the University of North Florida and Concordia University. She holds a PhD in Educational Leadership Policy and Human Development from North Carolina State University, a master's degree in Occupational and Technical Studies, emphasis HR-Training from Old Dominion University, and a bachelor's degree in Business Education from NC A&T State University.

Michelle Bartlett, PhD, assistant professor at Old Dominion University, teaching in the Community College Leadership and Workforce and Organizational Development doctoral programs. She received her PhD in Higher Education Leadership with a cognate in Statistics from Clemson University. In addition to her academic role, Dr. Bartlett consults with higher education, healthcare, government, and workforce organizations on executive leadership training and capacity building. She is editor of the *Journal of Apprenticeship and Work-Based Learning* and currently serves as the Professional Development Trustee for the Association of Career and Technical Education Research. Dr. Bartlett shares her passion for training design as the co-founder of the UNITE Collaborative Intelligence Lab.

Workforce Blueprint

A Framework for Scaling Talent in Industry

Leressa Suber and Michelle Bartlett

Routledge
Taylor & Francis Group
NEW YORK AND LONDON

Designed cover image: Getty Images

First published 2027
by Routledge
605 Third Avenue, New York, NY 10158

and by Routledge
4 Park Square, Milton Park, Abingdon, Oxon, OX14 4RN

Routledge is an imprint of the Taylor & Francis Group, an informa business

Library of Congress Cataloging-in-Publication Data
Names: Suber, Leressa author | Bartlett, Michelle E., 1974– author
Title: Workforce blueprint : a framework for scaling talent in industry / Leressa Suber and Michelle Bartlett.
Description: New York, NY : Routledge, 2026. | Includes bibliographical references and index.
Identifiers: LCCN 2026009441 (print) | LCCN 2026009442 (ebook) | ISBN 9781032849812 hardback | ISBN 9781032836362 paperback | ISBN 9781003515937 ebook
Subjects: LCSH: Manufacturing industries—Personnel management | Construction industry—Personnel management | Diversity in the workplace
Classification: LCC HD9720.5 .S83 2026 (print) | LCC HD9720.5 (ebook) | DDC 658.3—dc23/eng/20260604
LC record available at https://lccn.loc.gov/2026009441
LC ebook record available at https://lccn.loc.gov/2026009442

ISBN: 978-1-032-84981-2 (hbk)
ISBN: 978-1-032-83636-2 (pbk)
ISBN: 978-1-003-51593-7 (ebk)

DOI: 10.4324/9781003515937

Typeset in Sabon
by Apex CoVantage, LLC

Contents

Acknowledgements

The development and completion of this book have been made possible through the collaboration and support of many leading practitioners, technical experts, and field leaders. We greatly appreciate your time and contributions to our work.

We want to express our sincere appreciation to the publishing team, whose strategic insight, editorial expertise, and commitment to excellence ensured the highest professional standards in every stage of this project.

We are grateful for the Subject Matter Experts (SMEs) whose lived experiences, thoughtful discussions, and relevant perspectives helped enhance the knowledge, skills, and practical examples presented throughout the chapters. We are thankful to the organizations that provided access to data, case studies, and real-world insights, enriching the depth and relevance of this work.

Finally, we must acknowledge our family and friends for their support and encouragement throughout this process. Thank you to all of our family who jumped in to read chapters and make suggestions throughout the journey. Your participation was so incredibly valuable.

Subject Matter Experts (SMEs)

Iyioluwa Adesan, Apprentis Co-founder (UK)
Kevin Blount, President, SAFECO Inc.
Nicholas D'Antonio, PhD, Project Engineering Manager, Aerospace and Defense
Miranda Dalton, Program Manager, Economic Development
Tameka Davis, SHRM-CP, HR Director
John DiDio, Former Director of the EEOC (local Virginia office)
Alaina Doyle, PhD, Flourish Coaching and Consulting
Wendell T. Green, AIA, Owner, WTG Design Architects, LLC
Brandon Hensley, Dean of CTE at McDowell Technical Community College

Adrianne Kroll, Founder, EdgeFactory AI
Nathan Mark, Superintendent, Construction Development Services Inc
John McMahon, Internal Editor
Bolu Olawaye, Apprentis Co-founder (UK)
Taylor Rodriguez, PhD, Internal Editor
Ellysa Smith, CuraHuman

Introduction

The pandemic and automation changed *"how" we work, "where" we work, "what" work we do, and "who" will do the work*. The cumulative uncertainty has further decreased talent pipelines, particularly within technical industries such as manufacturing, construction, and engineering. These talent shortages have impacted business productivity and performance. Businesses are challenged to continually improve innovation, creativity, and competitive advantage. Research indicates that prioritizing representation improves engagement in global markets. To meet these demands, employers should examine HR practices to attract, recruit, and retain racially and ethnically diverse talent. This book will examine the history of diversity management, elements of talent management, and HR practices (strategic, development, and operational) that contribute to recruitment and retention, as well as key stakeholders involved in building diverse talent pipelines. While the book is based on general technical industries, with a few highlighted, the content can be applied widely across all industries. The goal is to provide a comprehensive, practical guide to building diverse talent that can be immediately applied to address talent shortages.

What Is the Book's Foundation

The book is based on Dr. Leressa Suber's dissertation, entitled "Manufacturing Small Business Case Study: Successful HR Practices for Recruiting and Retaining Racially and Culturally Diverse Talent," which chronicles two small and medium-sized enterprises that employ fewer than 150 people. From that dissertation, the authors have developed an action-oriented practitioner-focused framework to assist HR practitioners, business owners, and policymakers on how to expand talent in technical industries. The Talent Expansion Framework (TXF) will be introduced as a model for shaping the future of work through intentional actions by leadership, community, and employees.

DOI: 10.4324/9781003515937-1

The data shared throughout this book are from case studies and individuals' reflections from subject matter experts (SMEs), HR practitioners, and owners in construction, manufacturing, and engineering.

Who the Book Is For

As academic scholars and practitioners in the fields that intersect education, HR, and the workforce, we are uniquely positioned to share qualitative and quantitative outcomes. We include real-life case studies, SME perspectives, tips, lessons learned, and implications for future exploration. The book provides actionable steps that business owners, HR practitioners, and policymakers can take to support the development of a diverse workforce, encompassing company branding, community engagement/partnerships, training, and organizational culture considerations. Although this book is written as an off-the-shelf, daily resource for practitioners, it can be embedded in course curricula to expand upon concepts taught in business, HR development (HRD), and HR certification programs. This book can be read individually for personal growth and development, or as part of an informal, self-directed professional development program for leaders in any organization.

How the Book Is Organized

The book contains 11 chapters. We begin by setting the stage in Chapter 1, which introduces the rationale for the book and its components, and in Chapter 2, we address how to navigate talent management in the new future of work. Our discussion on "Recruitment" includes five chapters that address a strategic approach to recruitment, including leadership influence and community engagement, as well as an understanding of the talent in technical industries. Then, we address "Retention," including development and operational practices that influence retention. Finally, Chapter 11 presents future directions for work in technical industries, including leadership reflections, policy changes, and recommendations for the future of work.

Throughout each chapter, the book is organized to grab quick, bite-sized key points, SME quotes, and other applicable connections/resources for strengthening HR practices across organizations. The book can be read cover to cover (which we highly recommend) or based on specific workforce needs. To inform readers' interest and engagement, a synopsis of each chapter is provided at the end of the introduction. To simplify key points, a legend is included below to help HR practitioners guide talent expansion.

HR Action Steps

Throughout the book, the authors have labeled key action steps for business owners, HR practitioners, middle managers, and others to help diversify and expand talent pipelines. The HR action steps section outlines the guiding principles, actions, and the company contributors responsible for implementing them.

SME Reflections

To reinforce action steps, the authors provide real-world accounts and experiences of SMEs in the field. The SMEs highlighted will share their perspectives, key lessons learned, and best practices for implementing action steps. During these reflections, you will see cameos of industry leaders, along with key quotes or recommendations based on their experiences.

Authors' Tips

The authors will provide tips for overcoming barriers or challenges to advancing recommendations, as appropriate, throughout the chapters. While action steps are necessary to expand talent pipelines, understanding how to overcome issues along the way is necessary to ensure implementation and sustainability.

Chapter Conclusions

Since the book is structured for individual and collective chapter reading, the chapter conclusions offer distinct, action-oriented opportunities to guide your planning and implementation. Some chapters expand on forward thinking through lists of action steps; others provide strategies or tools for putting concepts into practice; and some offer reflective questions for considering individual and organizational impact.

Resources

With any practical guide, multiple resources are available to accomplish objectives, goals, and outcomes. Throughout the book, various websites, resources, and organizations that offer additional information will be highlighted.

Chapter Synopsis

Chapter 1: Framing Technical Industries

This chapter identifies the key elements that shape our approach to unlocking talent and developing a framework for enhancing talent in technical industries. It highlights technical industries and the past, current, and future states of manufacturing, construction, and engineering. Additionally, it examines how HR professionals are addressing changing trends, as well as how long-term employees in technical industries are adapting to these changes. A framework to address how to unlock talent in technical industries, referred to as "the Talent Expansion Framework (TXF)" for technical industries, is introduced.

Chapter 2: Talent Management and Technology Advancement

This chapter examines how technological advancements, particularly those associated with the Fourth Industrial Revolution, are transforming talent management in technical industries, including manufacturing, engineering, and construction. It emphasizes the need for a comprehensive workforce development strategy to address the skills gap created by automation, artificial intelligence, and digital transformation. The chapter emphasizes the importance of collaboration among educational institutions, employers, and policymakers in creating a workforce ecosystem that can adapt to these changes. It also emphasizes the importance of adopting diverse and inclusive hiring practices to attract underrepresented groups, including women, minorities, veterans, and immigrants, thereby securing a competitive advantage. By leveraging technology and human-centered approaches, HR professionals can navigate the future of work, foster innovation, and meet the evolving demands of a global workforce. The chapter provides actionable strategies for talent acquisition, retention, and development that align workforce skills with industry needs.

Chapter 3: Building on Origins of Talent Opportunity

This chapter explains how practice has evolved beyond affirmative action to focus on building strong teams through everyday management. It argues that compliance alone misses today's labor market realities and urges practical strategies across the talent pipeline, including recruitment, retention, and development, specifically in technical fields. The focus shifts from policy checklists to performance drivers. Emphasis on clear hiring and advancement criteria, skills-based pathways, targeted mentoring, and work environments can enable collaboration and problem-solving, thereby boosting innovation and competitiveness while keeping opportunities tied to ability and potential.

Chapter 4: Leadership Influence on Recruitment

This chapter examines how leaders shape the effectiveness of recruitment across the entire talent pipeline. It demonstrates how leaders directly influence recruitment quality by establishing clear standards, exemplifying fair and skills-based hiring practices, and aligning talent decisions with business objectives. It outlines a practical framework that leaders can drive with HR, including workforce planning and setting clear roles and skills profiles to ensure qualified sourcing and talent retention. Drawing on executive examples, it emphasizes leaders' visible participation in interview calibration, the removal of process bottlenecks, and regular funnel reviews that hold teams accountable for their results. The chapter concludes by emphasizing the importance of sustained executive ownership as a competitive advantage, facilitating faster and better hires, and establishing the conditions for new employees to contribute and grow.

Chapter 5: Strategic HR Practices for Recruitment

This chapter explores the critical role of strategic human resource management in attracting and retaining talent. It emphasizes the importance of aligning recruitment practices with an organization's mission, vision, and core values to meet the evolving demands of automation and technology. The chapter highlights the significance of leadership in driving diversity efforts and recommends a focus on leadership identity, style, and commitment to fostering an inclusive workforce. It also discusses change management strategies for integrating diversity into recruitment processes, particularly in technical industries. Key topics include assessing organizational readiness for diversity, engaging with communities, and integrating diversity into the organizational culture. By adopting intentional recruitment strategies and building a strong foundation of inclusive practices, organizations can improve performance, retention, and innovation. The chapter concludes with action steps to enhance recruitment planning, including leveraging diverse networks, fostering internal referrals, and ensuring inclusive communication throughout the hiring process.

Chapter 6: Community Engagement and Partnership Roles in Recruitment

This chapter underscores the importance of community engagement and partnerships in recruiting diverse talent. It emphasizes the need for organizations to immerse themselves in local communities, working with schools, churches, nonprofits, and workforce development agencies to build strong, diverse talent pipelines. The chapter provides actionable steps for employers to engage with minority-serving institutions, veterans, and other underrepresented groups. By creating alliances with community partners, companies can expand their recruitment reach and become more visible to diverse populations. The chapter also highlights the benefits of collaborative efforts with economic development agencies, chambers of commerce, and other conveners to strengthen recruitment and retention efforts. Overall, community engagement is presented as a critical strategy for addressing talent shortages and building a more inclusive workforce.

Chapter 7: Targeting Special Populations for Recruitment

This chapter focuses on strategies for recruiting underrepresented groups, including women, minorities, veterans, and individuals with disabilities, particularly in technical industries. It emphasizes the importance of tailoring recruitment efforts to address the unique challenges these special populations face. The chapter discusses approaches such as targeted outreach, partnerships with community organizations, and modifying job descriptions to be more inclusive. By implementing these strategies, companies can tap into diverse talent pools, improving workforce diversity and filling critical roles in industries facing labor shortages. The chapter encourages organizations to adopt flexible and innovative recruitment methods to attract and retain talent from these special populations.

Chapter 8: Tactical HR Practices: Training Programs for Retention

This chapter emphasizes the importance of training and development as HR practices for retaining talent, particularly in technical industries such as manufacturing, construction, and engineering. As automation and technology advance, training becomes crucial for preparing the workforce to meet new skill demands. HR Development practices are framed as proactive, addressing the war for talent and the need for companies to stay competitive globally. The chapter explores how training programs act as strategic levers, promoting inclusivity and career advancement across diverse employee groups. It also discusses apprenticeship programs, leadership development, and equitable access to professional growth. The focus is on creating inclusive, tailored training plans and internal mentorship programs that enhance retention while fostering diversity. By addressing the talent shortage and ensuring equitable training opportunities, organizations can build a future-ready, inclusive workforce capable of competing in the global economy.

Chapter 9: Operational HR Practices: Considerations for Retention

This chapter emphasizes the vital role of employee feedback in enhancing retention strategies. It explores how actively listening to employees and incorporating their input into HR practices can lead to increased job satisfaction and reduced turnover, as well as various methods for gathering feedback, such as surveys, focus groups, and one-on-one interviews, while stressing the importance of creating a culture where employees feel heard and valued are detailed. Beyond feedback mechanisms, the chapter highlights the critical role of leadership in shaping people-centered operational practices. It examines how leaders' values, communication styles, and day-to-day interactions directly influence employee engagement, trust, and long-term retention. Particular attention is given to communication as a core operational strategy, including interpersonal, intercultural, and digital approaches that support inclusive and effective workplace interactions. The chapter also considers how organizational size and hierarchy impact the implementation of HR practices, noting that flexibility, visibility, and relationship building are especially important in small to medium-sized organizations. Ultimately, it reinforces that retention is not driven by policy alone, but by consistent, intentional leadership behaviors and operational practices that prioritize employee experience, strengthen trust, and foster a sense of belonging across the organization.

Chapter 10: Employee Voices Amplify Retention

This chapter highlights the critical role of employee voice in strengthening retention in today's competitive workforce. Organizations must move beyond traditional approaches and instead prioritize listening to and acting on employee feedback. The chapter illustrates how feedback can inform HR strategic, development, and operational practices, improving job satisfaction and organizational culture. Using the employee-focused component of the Talent Expansion Framework (TXF), it offers a structured approach for integrating employee perspectives into decision-making, engagement, and recognition. By emphasizing continuous dialogue, transparency, and responsiveness, the chapter positions employee feedback as a key driver of trust, belonging, and long-term retention, providing practical strategies for leaders to build more responsive and sustainable workplaces.

Chapter 11: Reflections and Recommendations for Talent Expansion

This chapter examines the leadership implications for the future of work, particularly in technical industries such as manufacturing. It offers insights into how talent expansion will shape the broader economy and the evolving labor market. The chapter also provides recommendations and reflections on leadership identity and styles in talent development. Emphasizing the need for forward-thinking strategies, it urges leaders, policymakers, and organizations to prioritize reflexivity as a crucial component of future workforce success, thereby ensuring a competitive advantage and driving innovation in a rapidly changing world.

Authors' Note

As scholar-practitioners, we conduct research that requires us to address our identity as scholars, our "positionality." Building positionality statements goes beyond just helping the readers understand who we are (our biographies) and addresses who we are as researchers and why doing this work matters to us. Although this book is intended for scholar-practitioners and is not written through a research lens, we believe it is valuable for you to understand us as researchers, scholars, practitioners, and, most importantly, as people. We hope the following introductions provide a deeper context for who we are, our work, and the purpose behind our development of the Workforce Blueprint. As true architects of this work, we recognize that our lived experiences and ongoing works bring value to the book. A meaningful exploration of a topic of this magnitude requires grace, trust, and space to impart knowledge and wisdom. We do not take your willingness to read our work lightly. We value your time, energy, and experience. The strategies, tips, and tools are offered as mechanisms to spark inspiration, motivation, and activation for this work. We hope this book provides you with new insights, a pause for reflection, and shared discourse with other scholars, practitioners, researchers, students, policymakers, employers, and more. Thank you for your time.

Leressa R. Suber, PhD, PHR, SHRM-CP

Leressa Suber holds a PhD from North Carolina State University in Educational Leadership Policy and Human Development, emphasizing workforce development, a master's degree in Occupational and Technical Studies, emphasis HR-Training from Old Dominion University, and a bachelor's degree in Business Education from NC A&T State University. Leressa Suber is Principal Consultant of Bonsai Consulting Group, a firm focused on research, coaching, and evaluation of workforce development, STEM, and leadership development programs. She has led HR operations, evaluated federally funded workforce and STEM initiatives, and advised organizations on leadership and HR development. Her work is distinguished by her ability to connect talent strategy, workforce systems, education and evaluation to build a future-ready workforce.

Michelle E. Bartlett, PhD

Michelle Bartlett received her master's degree in Human Resource Education from the University of Louisville and her PhD in Higher Education

Leadership from Clemson University, with a cognate in Statistics. Currently, she is an assistant professor at Old Dominion University, teaching in both the Community College Leadership and Workforce and Organizational Development doctoral programs. Prior to her role at ODU, she worked at North Carolina State University, where she led the master's in Training and Development, co-led the doctoral program in Community College Leadership, and served as Coordinator of Competency-Based Education Initiatives for the College of Education. Michelle was the past editor of the *Career and Technical Education Research* (CTER) journal. She currently serves as the Professional Development Trustee for the Association for Career and Technical Education Research. Michelle shares her passion for inclusive training design as the co-founder of the UNITE Collaborative Intelligence Lab.

Disclaimer: AI Technology and Reference List

The authors acknowledge the use of AI technology in checking for grammar (e.g., Grammarly). ChatGPT was used as a tool in early-stage development for idea exploration. It did not contribute substantive text, analysis, or conclusions.

Chapter 1

Framing Technical Industries

Technical industries require highly tactile skills and involve producing or transporting goods and services. Previously known in education settings as industries requiring vocational skills, these industries place a strong emphasis on occupation-specific competencies. These competencies typically take a practical, applied approach to learning, which can be observed and implemented in an on-the-job environment. When workers can translate these skill sets to tasks within an industry, they have employability skills. The Organisation for Economic Co-operation and Development presents manufacturing, engineering, and construction as an occupational cluster in their 2024 Programme for International Student Assessment (PISA) Vocational Education Training (VET) Initiative. A brief overview of each industry is highlighted below to add context to the current state of the industries. We will address the differences in "where" we work as technology transforms the work environment later in the chapter. Within the US, technical roles have typically been filled through vocational programs offered at two-year community colleges, vocational skills training, and apprenticeship programs. We focus on three technical industries (manufacturing, engineering, and construction) because these areas are experiencing the most significant talent shortages and represent sectors that propel the United States' competitive advantage forward.

SME Perspectives from the Field

As part of our research, we interviewed several individuals in manufacturing, construction, and engineering to establish their perceptions of the changing trends and cultural environment related to the technological changes in their respective fields. From those interviews, we selected excerpts to introduce and reinforce keys concepts that mirror and inform our research.

DOI: 10.4324/9781003515937-2

Manufacturing

Manufacturing remains the heart of US jobs, with 12.7 million people employed in the field as of 2022.[1] However, the manufacturing industry has seen the largest uptick in technological changes across all industries. Automation has introduced various technologies to the manufacturing plant floor. These changes have not only shifted the skills required for project managers but also introduced new roles in maintenance, repair, and robotics. Technology has such a profound influence on the field that new equipment and operators have been required to oversee, operate, and repair items equipped with innovative technologies. New Industry 4.0 technologies include cloud computing, the Internet of Things, robotics, and other advanced technologies. Specific innovative manufacturing technologies utilize equipment and data analysis tools to simplify tasks, enhance safety, and improve efficiency.

When speaking with manufacturing field workers who plan to retire from the field, they offered the following historical context. The tools and instruments used in manufacturing were improved through computerized devices such as micrometers. The systems enhance tools and instruments, making them more effective and efficient, thereby reducing costs and staff workload. For example, a traditional drafter provides an angle for direction but cannot give specifics to determine the part. With the new technology, this is now possible. "Do more with less time and ease the production of finished products" is the message in the new digital age. The latest technological inventions have reduced the time spent in school and provided greater access for women to enter the field.

Talent Expansion by Gender Roles

Although gender roles have been a pain point in technical industries, with women's lack of representation and interest in the field, one respondent offered this insight into how technology is indirectly contributing to female participation in the field:

> I recall when one female knew how to make the blueprint for the machine to create the part, but [she] had never been to the machine shop. She was able to create the blueprint. This improved access to the field through computer training, but it was no longer necessary to physically manufacture the product. Before the introduction of computers and technology into the field, geometry was used to determine the appropriate angles for assembling parts, as opposed to computerized blueprints. Today, in some industries, computer designers perform this work. They do not know how to drill holes at all, and they don't need to.

Real-World Example of Downsizing

To address concerns related to changing skill sets and downsizing, the same respondent provided the following illustrations during his work. "All three machines on the factory floor followed the exact blueprint. With each machine upgrade, workforce sections were eliminated. The final machine upgrade had the most significant and efficient impact on the workforce." He explained the ratio of machine transition to job loss as follows:

> One machine required three people, but it eliminated nine jobs. Then, with the next machine upgrade, 12 jobs were lost. Eventually, a whole shift of workers was eliminated. Continuous upgrades cause delays. Within two years, they sent their work to the home office and eliminated an entire southern unit.

Reflections on Changing Times of Manufacturing

In the 1990s, technological changes were made manually by retrofitting multiple machines to create a single prototype machine that could do it "all." One respondent recounts the following:

> Machinery upgrades were implemented manually over time, resulting in the elimination of 2000 jobs over a short-period of time. Specifically, six machines that performed the same functions were manually disassembled, and their parts were reassembled to create a single, efficient, stand-alone machine.

Today, no retrofitting occurs; all robotic applications perform this function. The troubleshooting of applications occurs through lighting up, dropping, pre-fabrication, and hooking it up. Therefore, the time to fix machines has been significantly reduced, both mechanically and in productivity time.

During this time, familiar relationships and referrals significantly influenced standard recruitment practices in manufacturing. Typically, one respondent we interviewed (who had worked in electrical manufacturing for over 20 years) recalls jewelers and watchmakers who followed this path. He noted that historically other countries employed an unskilled labor force, as seen in the textile industries of foreign countries. He marveled at how today all countries are contributing to technological advancements. For example, he emphasized the production of cellular and chip technologies

Where Do We Work?

A respondent recounts where and how he used to work in manufacturing:

> In the past, manufacturing companies in the northern United States were outfitted with more new tools, while companies in the southern United

States often received used or "hand me down" machinery and equipment. Therefore, workers may have had new, old, or mixed equipment to perform the task. Older equipment took longer to complete tasks, and those whom [leaders] felt were more qualified got better equipment. Additionally, the factory floor was often hot and dirty. The workers were responsible for cleaning their spaces, and relying on long aprons to help keep their clothes clean.

How We Work?

In the 1980s, the manufacturing environment required workers to monitor your learning environment and show you how to do the work. The equipment and safety protocols were strict and required you to walk through the process with a journeyman. "Often, this created hostile working conditions, like a rite of passage, to become a trainee. There was a gatekeeping of knowledge of information throughout the journeyman process."

As the only minority (African American/Black male) among 30 workers in his department, he faced challenges. "Dealing with the power hierarchy was the most difficult, moving from difficult guys every three months. They did not give me the knowledge to succeed: they were going to make sure I didn't go any higher than journeyman." He says "today schools are better, informing you that the curriculum is more up-to-date, and you see parallel experiences to the workplace. In night school, it was not that way. There was only book learning, versus the hands-on approach that exists today. Instead of practical experiences, you ventured off on field trip experiences to observe but did not have access to the hands-on learning." Similarly, "the journeyman (whom we apprenticed under) was supposed to let you borrow their tools, or you had to have your own tools. At some companies, a salesperson would come in, and the company would buy tools for you directly." The company would deduct the cost of tools from your paycheck. Inequitable practices, such as nepotism, in which some people would receive their tools for free, were prevalent.

Engineering

Engineering, the heart of STEM (science, technology, engineering, and math), is the top career field to pursue for the highest entry-level income. However, technology is impacting how engineers design, develop, and implement processes. As traditional degree programs are being sidelined in favor of less time-consuming and engaging learning, the field needs to adapt to meet the world's needs. From our interviews with engineers, a consistent theme emerged: Design work is a process of deep thinking paired with uncompromising attention to safety and evolving licensure requirements.

Reflections in Daily Life of Engineering

One interviewee explained, "It's one thing to put it on the paper, but you have to think about it. So, it might take three hours for you to think about it, and it takes you 10 minutes to put it down." This person emphasized that within engineering, "We're officers of safety first." The credentialing landscape reinforces continuous learning. "We in the profession have to do continuing education. For example, I have to do 18 hours of continuing education." Licensure itself is shifting. "There were nine parts to the exam. They have now squashed it into seven parts," and preparation now includes practice management. Today, some aspects of engineering require components of entrepreneurship. "They want you to be knowledgeable of how to run a business," including decisions such as "Do you set up a C Corp, or do you set up an S Corp?"

Demographic Composition of Engineering

The interviewees also underlined representation, scale, and early outreach. One participant noted, "In the Commonwealth of Virginia, there are only 86 Black registered architects." While generally demand is rising, supply remains constrained. As one put it, "We do not have enough engineers and architects." Quantitatively, "You have roughly about a million engineers," alongside targeted pipeline efforts that begin earlier. "You need to go to elementary schools and talk to elementary school kids and talk to young kids," supported by outreach, where "we have a career day for middle school kids."

Construction

A poor reputation and branding have hurt the construction industry. It also struggles with a lack of interest in pursuing a career in the field. More importantly, gender equality remains a point of contention. However, technologies are reducing the weight requirements for other physical job functions necessary for success in highly tactile roles. In this way, technology is helping decrease gender equity gaps by improving access and overall confidence in meeting job expectations.

Drawing on interviews with construction experts, we trace the evolution of the field's labor pipeline and practices from guild traditions to modern credentials and safety regimes. As one expert reminded us, "Apprenticeship in the construction industry has a long history," and those pathways still matter, even as "safety standards have improved over time," with basics like the "OSHA 10 class for construction and general industry" now commonplace. Together, the construction experts we spoke to describe a sector where hands-on learning, codified training, and steadily strengthened protections have shaped how people enter, advance, and stay safe on the job. They also emphasized the people and production realities that have long defined the workforce. "Immigrants are a huge part of the construction industry," one noted. At the same time, another explained that because "the work is seasonal, some workers will look to relocate to areas where the work is steady year-round," creating persistent churn. Looking ahead, they see technology changing where and how work happens. "A substantial shift to modular construction off-site"—even if "the transition will take decades"—will continue to recalibrate skill demands and workforce stability.

Changing Landscape for HR Professionals

HR professionals are undergoing a transition in the future of work. Across various fields, HR professionals are required not only to reimagine the learning and development space for staff but also to enhance it. They must also improve in areas such as data analytics, artificial intelligence, machine learning, and other rapidly advancing technologies. We are hopeful that this book will provide HR professionals with the strategies and tools to strengthen their workforce. We acknowledge that this new future of work represents a changing landscape of challenges for HR professionals. We know they, too, are experiencing significant gaps, challenges, and concerns about working at their full capacity.

To ground this book in lived practice, we interviewed HR experts and have woven their perspectives throughout. In interviews, HR leaders described a talent market characterized by constrained resources, evolving skill needs, and the need for clearer growth pathways. A nonprofit public-health HR leader noted that attracting candidates is difficult when a competitive salary is expected amidst the limited organizational resources. Even as many applicants "want to make an impact for the greater good." One practitioner noted "retention is also hindered because we are a lean organization and don't have set career paths." On the small-business/nonprofit consulting side, the primary recruiting hurdle is "a skills gap," alongside candidates' expectations for "total compensation packages." They noted, "keeping people engaged requires 'meaningful career pathways' and continuous 'upskilling' for 'newer jobs' and future planning." Both these HR leaders we spoke with are turning to technology for assistance. One approach involves using AI with job descriptions. In contrast, other approaches rely on Enterprise Resource Planning systems to assist with holistic, functional HR capabilities. Some examples of operational technologies to assist in HR will be addressed in Chapter 9. Both HR practitioners stressed the importance of sequence over silos, with the consultant cautioning that "the tendency is to focus or start with the recruitment piece" when building internal capacity, which can mean you "do not have to find talent" externally as often.

Talent Expansion Framework (TXF)

Framework Origin

To guide the process of building a Talent Expansion Framework (TXF), a framework based on real-world case studies[2] was adapted and expanded to address key factors that can strengthen talent shortages in technical industries. The first part of the framework is grounded in strategic, tactical, and operational HR practices, as initially emphasized in Shen et al.'s article, "Managing Diversity Through Human Resource Management: An International Perspective and Conceptual Framework."[3] It's significant to note that this article was published in an international journal, which highlights case studies from various countries, including Australia, Germany, and several African nations, among others. Although these cases were international, Dr. Suber's dissertation examined this framework among small manufacturing firms in the southern region of the United States (US). The organizations' focus on strategic, tactical, and operational aspects of diversity management serves as the basis for ensuring talent expansion. Despite critiques of diversity, equity, and inclusion (DEI) in this political context, adopting principles that align with improving diversity outcomes can profoundly enhance the ramifications of talent shortages and skills development in technical industries. Therefore, the new Talent Expansion Framework will be built upon these HR practices to ensure effective attraction, recruitment, and retention of a skilled workforce.

Developing and Applying the Framework

Dr. Leressa Suber's dissertation at North Carolina State University, entitled "Manufacturing Small Business Case Study: Successful HR Practices for Recruiting and Retaining Racially and Culturally Diverse Talent," focused on HR practices for attracting, recruiting, and retaining diverse talent in manufacturing. The dissertation involved two case studies on small and medium-sized enterprises (fewer than 150 employees) who were successful at expanding talent through diversity. Those case studies serve as an impetus for this book. Based on lessons learned in the dissertation and over 15 years of experience in human resources in the construction field, as well as in training community college leaders, the authors partnered to extend this work and develop a practical guide to help practitioners, policymakers, and employers build talent in technical industries.

The main elements of the Talent Expansion Framework, which are shown in Figure 1.1, focus on the strategic, development, and operational-level

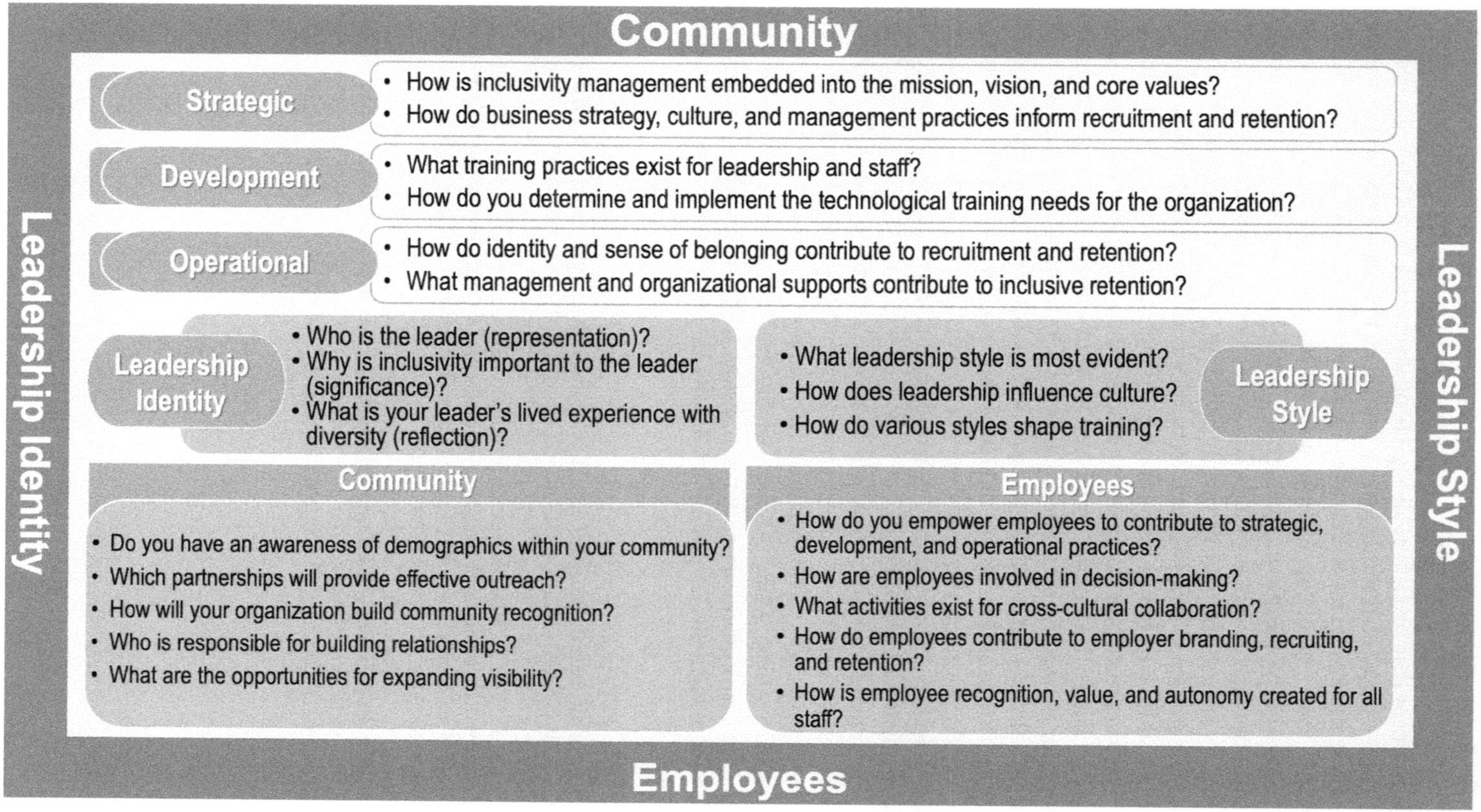

Figure 1.1 Talent Expansion Framework (TXF). Image Credit: Laurel A. Royer (2026)

HR practices that strengthen all aspects of diverse talent within organizations. The other areas of the framework represent the actors that contribute to applying the principles within the organization. For example, leaders, specifically their leadership identity and style, contribute to their approach to diversity management. Interactions with the community (educational institutions, partnerships, nonprofits, grassroots organizations) provide an outlet to attract and recruit talent. Similarly, past and present employees have a significant influence on recruitment and retention. Each of these areas will be covered in its respective chapter, along with its contribution to the attraction, recruitment, and selection of talent. Prompting questions in Figure 1.1 enable employers to gain a deeper understanding and vision for expanding their talent pipelines. The framework acts as a lever to unlock talent in extraordinary places and spaces. This book offers valuable insights, tools, and resources to help mobilize a new workforce in technical industries. We offer this framework as a guide to a practical application that addresses "how to do," "when to do," and "who will do" aspects of recruitment and retention.

The remainder of the book will focus on elements of the TXF and how it can be applied across industries. By answering questions within the core of the framework, the authors will address how talent can be expanded in technical sectors. While the basis of this framework was developed with an emphasis on diversity expansion, it has evolved to address all areas of talent management, ensuring both depth and breadth of talent expansion.

Notes

1 Bureau of Labor Statistics (2023, October). Retrieved from https://www.bls.gov/opub/ted/2023/a-look-at-manufacturing-jobs-on-national-manufacturing-day.htm
2 Suber, L. (2023). Manufacturing Small Business Case Study: Successful HR Practices for Recruiting and Retaining Racially and Culturally Diverse Talent. [Doctoral dissertation, North Carolina State University]. NCSU Campus Library. https://catalog.lib.ncsu.edu/catalog/NCSU5800793
3 Shen, J., Chanda, A., D'Netto, B., and Monga, M. (2009). Managing Diversity Through Human Resource Management: An International Perspective and Conceptual Framework. *The International Journal of Human Resource Management,* 20(2), 235–251. https://doi.org/10.1080/09585190802670516

Chapter 2

Talent Management and Technology Advancement

Technology is impacting talent management. Talent management is the HR function that implements practices to attract, recruit, develop, and retain top talent within a specified field. This chapter provides an overview of navigating the technological advancements that exist, including the who, what, when, where, and why for each technical area. Chapters 3–7 will establish a foundation for expanding talent in technical industries through strategic, leadership, and partnership-based involvement. Chapters 8–10 will focus on retaining the technical workforce, including operational and development practice. In the final chapter, authors provide reflection and recommendations for the future of talent expansion.

Impact of Technological Advancements on Talent Management

According to the US Department of Labor, workforce development ensures employers have qualified candidates to meet workforce needs (i.e., knowledge, skills, abilities).[1] Historically, extreme technological changes have drastically impacted working conditions. The Industrial Revolutions carved out unique challenges for workforce education and development. Progressions through Industry 1.0 (mechanical engineering), Industry 2.0 (electrical power), and Industry 3.0 (computer- and internet-enabled technologies) created the momentum for advances beyond previous technological limitations.[2] Today, continuous modern technological advances have ushered in the Fourth Industrial Revolution, known as Industry 4.0, which involves the integration of various digital technologies, including the Internet of Things (IoT), augmented reality, automation, and machine learning.

Although technology acts as a catalyst for positive impacts, the workforce development system is struggling to meet the needs of employers in technical industries. The expansion of talent pipelines and identification

DOI: 10.4324/9781003515937-3

of new skill requirements continue to be a setback to industry production and human performance. The United States (US) must intentionally shift its educational systems, training mechanisms, and funding to upskill its workforce. This overhaul of the workforce system will require an all-hands-on-deck approach, including all educational levels (K–12), community colleges, four-year institutions, employers, and political support. Collaboration among workforce system entities and partnerships is referred to as a workforce development ecosystem. Therefore, situating the workforce ecosystem that strengthens and promotes technical industries will better position the US for a global competitive advantage. Our Talent Expansion Framework (TXF) outlines the key components that serve as a model for unlocking talent.

As the pandemic has altered the working environments of the workforce, the boundaries between work and personal life have blurred, with many people recalibrating obligations prioritizing their personal lives over their careers. As the world becomes more comfortable with the state of the industry, other countries are surpassing the US in preparedness to meet shifting technological advancements. Although other countries were previously reluctant to adopt technologies due to the high cost of equipment and training, many countries, including Germany, Australia, and the United Kingdom, are making this shift through training trend changes, such as the increase in internships, externships, and apprenticeship programs (discussed in Chapter 8).

In the US, employers and HR managers should make a conscious effort to ensure their workforce is not intimidated by how technology will transform current roles within their organizations. Instead, they must take specific steps to reinforce confidence in staff knowledge and skill sets. Initially, it was thought that the first line of impact of automation would be low-wage roles. However, roles throughout organizations, including C-suite leadership, management, and staff, are impacted by technological advancements, such as generative artificial intelligence (Gen AI). Gen AI refers to tools and applications that use large language models (LLMs), including ChatGPT, Gemini, and others. These shifts require HR practitioners to possess the skills necessary to lead technology change and ensure effective implementation through human resource development (HRD) activities, such as instructional design, leadership development, and coaching. To ensure transparency in the promotion and advancement of the new role, changes will be required across job design, skill development, and knowledge transfer. Research indicates that artificial intelligence is embedded in talent management practices, where data analysis automatically assesses productivity issues. For example, at Amazon warehouses, over 300 employees were terminated for failure to meet performance measures.[3]

Although the progression of technologies has maximized our ability to perform complex tasks, the talent and skills required to meet this change are not keeping pace with trends. Industry 4.0, characterized by automation, has changed *"how" we work, "where" we work, "what" work we do, "when" we work, and "who" does the work.* Although all industries are experiencing talent shortages, technical industries are experiencing massive attrition in record numbers. Today, 7.2 million jobs in the US have been impacted by automation, negatively affecting technical industries such as manufacturing, engineering, and construction.[4] While this book provides evidence on recruitment within these industries, the action steps highlighted apply to every industry.

Current State of the Workforce

Historically, the White population represented the largest composition of the US groups. However, in the last 20 years, its share of the overall population decreased by 10 percent. By 2045, the White population is expected to become a minority as the overall population increases.[5] According to the most recent data from the Bureau of Labor Statistics, 58 percent of the workforce is White. Other underrepresented populations (e.g., Hispanic/Latinx, Black/African American, and Asian) are increasing in representation, with each group making up 12–18 percent of the workforce.[6]

As the composition of the workforce changes, strategies to train and upskill new talent emerge as a top priority for organizations. Within post-secondary education, enrollments for underrepresented populations are increasing, and opportunities for short bursts of learning through community college programs, certificates, and other programs are experiencing an infusion of funding through various state, local, and federal grant programs.

This shift will present challenges for organizations with predominantly White and male workforces, as demographic trends indicate a more diverse labor pool entering these fields, requiring organizations to adapt their recruitment, retention, and workplace culture strategies to remain competitive. By understanding how to attract, recruit, and retain talent effectively, HR practitioners will be well-positioned to compete in both domestic and international markets. Despite the inherent need for this intentional shift to unlock talent across demographics, the US is experiencing setbacks due to its political system. The negative backlash from these requirements has created a bullseye on diversity, equity, and inclusion. At the time of this writing, intentional efforts to strengthen diverse organizations were under attack, resulting in job losses, increased retirements, and triggering unemployment for many individuals. It is too early to determine the impact these changes will have on long-term workforce demand, forecasting, employment outcomes, and mental health and wellness among workers. However, we believe the content addressed in this book will make meaningful contributions to strengthening the technical workforce and increasing the talent pipelines necessary for competitive growth among employers.

Transforming Perspectives on Technology

Technical industries provide access to high-quality jobs with minimal entry requirements and quick advancement through the occupational hierarchy. More importantly, these roles offer financial stability for long-term, gainful employment that can lead to retirement. Despite robust opportunities, ease of access, and financial gain, these industries struggle to attract top talent.

Historically, these industries were known for unsafe, unclean, back-breaking work. For example, in the early 20th century, coal miners faced constant threats of cave-ins, black lung disease, and explosions, while factory workers endured 12-hour shifts in poorly ventilated facilities with dangerous machinery and little to no safety equipment. Similarly, steel mill workers labored in extreme heat near molten metal with minimal protective gear, regularly suffering severe burns and injuries from flying sparks and heavy equipment. Construction workers on skyscrapers and bridges worked at dizzying heights without safety harnesses or reliable scaffolding, leading to frequent falls and fatalities. Shipyard welders and metal workers were exposed to toxic fumes and asbestos without proper ventilation or respiratory protection, resulting in long-term health consequences that often only appeared years later. However, technology has modernized working conditions within these fields. Unfortunately, the messaging around technical careers has not kept up with these changes.

Baby boomer retirements, poor industry reputations, and a lack of understanding about technological changes in modern work environments contribute to talent shortages. For example, technological changes compounded by the uncertainty of COVID have caused people from all walks of life to leave their traditional roles. However, this book will provide guidance and awareness for HR practitioners and educators within career and technical education programs to change the narrative around these fields in Chapter 6. Overall, a marketing campaign to educate K–12 populations, post-secondary educators, adults, and career changers will provide a boost to the talent necessary to ensure a competitive advantage across technical fields. While opportunities to engage an ecosystem of educational partners are addressed locally, statewide, and nationally through various workshops, conferences, and events, a formal consensus on how best to convene stakeholders, resources, and knowledge-sharing has not been reached.

Additionally, the infusion of artificial intelligence (AI), also known as generative artificial intelligence (Gen AI) through large language models (LLM) such as ChatGPT, Copilot, Gemini, Claude, and other solutions, continues to transform how we work in all industries. Specifically in technical industries, AI has been seen as both a strength and a detriment, as it will eliminate some jobs while extending other job functions, requiring new skill sets. In Chapter 8, a subject matter expert (SME) in embedding AI into technical industry settings provides insights and broad recommendations for technical industries.

Mobilizing a New Workforce

How should practitioners engage with new talent to meet the demands of the future of work? To fully mobilize a new and qualified workforce, HR practitioners must have a comprehensive understanding of the technical industries' landscape and the demographic composition of their current workforce. By undertaking this gap analysis, HR practitioners can assess their existing human resource management (HRM) practices and modify them to ensure all employees can confidently meet goals and maximize productivity and operational performance. More importantly, this analysis will enable practitioners to take intentional steps in building a diverse workforce capable of enhancing innovation and achieving a global competitive advantage.

The remainder of the chapter will focus on the landscape of technical industries, including (1) "how" we work, (2) "where" we work, (3) "when" we work, and (4) the demographic composition ("who" will do the work). It will provide an overview of the talent management activities needed to engage the workforce and how practitioners should respond to the changing needs of a diverse workforce.

The How: Strengthen the Human-Centric Connection

Technology changes the culture of work. HR professionals serve as a catalyst for connecting top talent with industry roles. An evaluation of HR best practices is necessary to identify and inventory the skills required to compete in 21st-century roles, such as manufacturing, engineering, construction, and other STEM-related fields. As we transition to automation and the future of work, mixed emotions about the impacts on the labor force exist. There are fears that technologies, including robots, will take over industries. We argue that human influence matters now more than ever before. People, including HR practitioners, should tap into their human-centric characteristics, such as emotional intelligence. We recognize that in a highly digitized, stressful world, it is the empathy and support of "people" that will enable Industry 4.0 transformation in technical industries. An empathetic "human connection" is the key to seamless implementation. Human resources (HR) functions necessary for successful digital transformation require a combined focus on HRM (recruitment, selection, staffing, and retention) and HRD (development and training). HR practitioners must cultivate human-centric connections by enhancing their emotional intelligence, active listening, and staying present, if staff feel comfortable confiding in them. More information about how leaders can engage in technical industries is provided in Chapter 4.

The Where: Change the Work Environment

Technology alters the physical environment in which we work and our interactions with the knowledge, skills, and abilities required to meet industry standards. In manufacturing factories, companies are shifting from manual tools and equipment to what is known as "smart manufacturing," a combination of digital technologies networked together to accomplish a set skill. For example, Sewbots® in the textile industry help produce products faster than those sewn by hand. This technology influences not only the skills but also the environmental conditions of the workplace. No longer are there images of "sweatshops" and people working long hours. Now, the textile industry is better equipped with robotic assistance for pattern-making, sewing, and cutting materials to get the best-quality product. Now, the work setting may be more attractive to other populations. For example, the traditional sewing roles have now been replaced by robots. Today, sewing can be done faster through working with co-robots. This is a process where women, men, and robots work together in harmony. A specific robot, known as a collaborative robot, will become a new co-worker in technical workspaces.

Many examples of technology changing workplace settings in construction and engineering are becoming consistently present and influential on productivity. Construction no longer requires onsite visits to make a bid or proposal on a new work project. Instead, technologies such as cameras, drones, Building Information Modeling (BIM), and high-definition 3D imaging can aid in the inspection of unsafe structures, including roofs, bridges, and tunnels.

The construction industry is undergoing rapid technological change. Technology can assist with a variety of tasks, including picking up heavy equipment, alleviating the need for weight restrictions within job requirements. Additionally, technology is reimagining how wiring is installed in homes. For example, electricians need to expand their skills to understand coding to ensure effective integration of smart home technologies. These technological adaptations may promote a more inclusive workplace. Specifically, these types of working conditions skill sets may now be more appealing for women, those with disabilities, and other populations who may not have otherwise considered construction or construction technology. Additionally, technological advances are creating parallel programs, such as smart homes and data warehouses, which provide opportunities for women to enter fields like construction, manufacturing, and engineering. For example, some community colleges are experiencing overwhelming enrollment in programs such as welding, construction, and engineering. Programs funded by community colleges involve cybersecurity, data analytics, and mechatronics (a blend of mechanical engineering and electronics). These skill sets are essential for working in various industries, particularly construction, engineering, and manufacturing.

The When: Scheduling the Work

Technology impacts work flexibility. Work no longer requires 24/7 access, as it no longer necessitates multiple people working 12-hour shifts. Robotics and innovative technologies enable workers in technical industries to refocus their efforts on the physical work environment (i.e., the factory floor, job site, lab) and concentrate on completing the work. For example, technology enables construction workers to use drones for site inspections, freeing up time for inspectors to examine other areas that require supervision or quality control. Moreover, the COVID-19 pandemic and the temporary transition to remote work have further exacerbated the talent shortage. This shift to remote work has catapulted the workforce into a new movement, where workers are demanding either fully remote work or hybrid opportunities. This concept, named the "great resignation" by Anthony Klotz, a psychologist and professor at Texas A&M University, reflects the massive and voluntary exodus of employees.[7] This workforce attrition is linked to a variety of reasons. Some voluntary exits are due to early retirement, shifts to second careers, and movement to global firms. Others include a failure to provide a work-life balance, as noted by the younger generations.

The Who: Demographic Composition

Age

The Organization for Economic Cooperation and Development (OECD) has documented shortages related to the aging population across the EU and the US, noting that in the US, people over 65 account for over 18.6

percent of the workforce.[8] Today, the technical industries attract multiple generations of workers, including baby boomers, millennials, and Generation Z. Discouraged by the pandemic and technological updates, baby boomers have been retiring in record numbers. However, for the older population that plan to stay, their roles deserve protection from early termination. Although all industries are at risk of perpetuating age discrimination, technical industries are more likely to remain biased due to the physical demands of these roles. HR managers and owners have a duty to ensure inclusive hiring across all age groups. In 2024, seven organizational cases were filed for violation of the Age Discrimination in Employment Act of 1967 (ADEA), which prohibits employment discrimination against people 40 years of age and older.[9] HR practitioners must create a culture that enables multiple generations of workers to coexist collaboratively, with all age groups feeling welcome and supported in achieving workplace goals. Multiple case studies support the use of multigenerational teams as a source of knowledge, capacity building, and value across generations and teams. Additionally, the introduction of technology through co-robots will provide beneficial outcomes. Research from multiple case studies indicates that strategies for promoting intergenerational work arrangements may be beneficial for strengthening performance. In the technological world, the introduction of co-robotics is a promising trend.

Race

According to the Pew Research Center (2018), African Americans and Latinx Americans combined make up 22 percent of the STEM workforce, while White Americans make up 69 percent.[10]

Since technical industries share skills with those in the STEM area, we will discuss underrepresented minorities in STEM as a starting point for recruitment across these industries. The current state of racial diversity in technical industries is minimal. Despite an intentional focus on improving racial underrepresentation in STEM fields, progress has been stagnant over the past 40 years. According to the National Science Foundation and the National Center for Science and Engineering Statistics, underrepresented students in STEM include the following demographics: Black, Hispanic, and American Indian and Alaska Native (AI/AN) populations.[11] Research indicates that contributors to underrepresentation in STEM include intrinsic feelings, as determined by "how industry conditions or personnel treat them," such as a lack of belonging, self-efficacy, and institutional support (e.g., mentoring, research experiences). Leading experts, such as Shaun Harper, PhD, a professor at the University of Southern California and a Forbes contributor, have developed frameworks to gain insights into what enables students of color to succeed in STEM fields.

Extrinsically, the workforce system has not been set up for the promotion and advancement of racially diverse candidates. Similarly, evidence supports that once underrepresented minorities enter the workforce, they do not see economic mobility or financial security at the same rates as their White counterparts. Equally, there are indications that some students who enter the field as early talent are involuntarily forced out due to social inequity, and the Washington Center for Equity Growth, and other scholarly researchers point to occupational segregation as an area to overcome in building workforce equity and equality.[12] Occupational segregation occurs when individuals of different ages and races are not equally represented in different kinds of jobs. For example, there may be a higher proportion of men in construction or more Hispanic individuals in entry-level roles in manufacturing. While more research is needed to determine how to advance talent among gender and underrepresented populations, throughout this book we will provide steps toward identifying gaps and taking action to facilitate change. If we continue to acknowledge a problem but fail to develop solutions, advancement will be stagnant. As technology advances, we must address systemic changes to ensure racial progress.

Immigrants

Prior to 1917, the immigrant population was not a highly regarded talent pool for work in many industries.[13] Immigrants endured similar treatment to non-White workers and were deemed inadequate for specific work duties. Today, the controversy over immigrant access to education and the workforce remains a volatile issue. Despite the pushback, research clearly demonstrates that immigrants will represent 82 percent of the workforce in the US by 2050.[14] Therefore, the time to address challenges to immigrant access to quality jobs is now. The red tape surrounding sponsorship for immigrants is both exhausting and requires a steep learning curve for owners and HR practitioners. Unfortunately, the political controversy continues to have a negative impact on immigrants as a talent resource. As political discourse and policies change, the rate at which this population engages in the US labor force may slow. HR practitioners and owners must consider how challenges to entry and workforce participation may exacerbate future talent pipelines and disrupt current operations.

Immigrants face obstacles to employment in technical industries, including documentation requirements, language barriers, inadequate transportation, and a lack of training to meet workforce needs. HR practitioners can play a pivotal role in outreach to this population. Their willingness to understand educational backgrounds, training capacities, and their engagement in technical industries will be instrumental in opening doors to immigrant populations. We provide more context to immigrant experiences in Chapter 7, where we discuss recruiting special populations.

Gender

Technical industries are predominantly male-driven. Therefore, intentional emphasis is necessary when considering women's advancement in these fields. By creating space for women to develop skills, advance, and lead, women may be more likely to consider these options. Research indicates that HR practices, including workplace flexibility, childcare support, mentor programs, and training opportunities are associated with increased support for women in technical industries such as manufacturing. The literature[15] includes the following examples:

DOW Chemical:

- Explores childcare partnerships and emphasizes mental well-being
- Uses structured mentoring programs like the Women Innovation Network (WIN)

Diamond Envelope, large manufacturing firm:

- Implements flexible scheduling with an "open-door" policy
- Shares women's success stories for recruitment

One research study suggests that effective HR practices can contribute to increased support for women in technical industries, such as manufacturing.[16] While women continue to experience discrimination and bias in male-dominated industries, intersectionality (race/gender/ability) should be another factor for consideration. Additional leadership styles and HR practices for strengthening HR skills will be discussed in Chapters 4 through 6. From an entry-level perspective, women are trailing in their access to technical fields. Several community colleges and four-year programs aim to attract women to STEM-related fields, but their programs of study often remain underrepresented in STEM fields in manufacturing and construction. More details on outreach will be discussed next.

Special Populations

As we consider the talent pool across technical industries, we must also consider populations from adjacent industries that possess skills complementary to those required. Special populations include veterans, special needs, including neurodiverse individuals, and justice-involved individuals. These groups may have worked in other industries, such as retail or automotive technology or not considered technical industries. Chapter 7 will address more information on special populations as a means of expanding talent pipelines.

VETERANS

Veterans transitioning into the workforce could potentially be untapped talent that has not been intentionally pursued. Based on prior learning assessments, veterans possess a range of skill sets that span multiple industries. The primary challenge facing veterans is their willingness to join organizations that lack a clear structure and defined career paths. Equally, employees struggle to translate their veteran skill sets into areas where they can contribute to the technical skills of the civilian workforce, such as airplane repair, artillery, or other highly technical fields specific to military operations. Many organizations, such as Operation Hero, Hire for America, and Wounded Warriors, are helpful in connecting the military to job opportunities. However, employers and HR practitioners require additional training on how to attract, recruit, and retain this population. Based on their profession, the veteran population potentially has access to the most technologically advanced training. Therefore, they can learn how to apply new skills to a civilian workforce if provided an equal opportunity to showcase their knowledge.

PERSONS WITH DISABILITY AND NEURODIVERGENCE

Prior to 2020, persons with a disability and neurodiverse populations had not been allowed the opportunity to prove their skills in technical industries. Many employers were fearful of the safety and/or legal ramifications of a person with a physical disability entering a hands-on work environment. More recently, several key case studies have demonstrated that individuals on the autism spectrum and others with visual or hearing impairments are capable of working in these environments, given simple modifications. According to Disability NC,[17] employers can provide cost-effective accommodation that fosters a mutually beneficial and positive work environment for both the employer and staff.

With regard to individuals who are neurodiverse, and those persons with an invisible disability, such as a learning disability (dyslexia), behavioral disability (ADHD), or other non-visible disability, may require shifts in workplace engagement. Additionally, mental health support services exist for those who may be experiencing mental health disorders, depression, and trauma (e.g., PTSD), which are reasonable and expected in technical industries as much as in other fields.

Other examples of best practices include partnering with organizations that work with special populations as part of the business model. The ability to build partnerships with local, state, and regional agencies to support workers and emerging programs ensures that non-duplicated services are provided. When employers develop partnerships that create, connect, and mobilize talent in key areas, they create mutual benefit and a win-win for the community at large. Below are a few examples of how to engage partners at the local, state, and national levels. We will provide a sample community immersion guide in Chapter 6.

- **Local Level:** Goodwill[18]
  Example of disability workforce assistance available through nonprofits.
- **State Level:** Excellence Training Center at Youngstown University[19]
  Example of workforce, education, research, and commercial centers offered through colleges and universities.
- **National Level:** Office of Disability Employment Policy[20]
  Example of governmental and other entities that offer disability-related technical assistance and guidance on policy development.

JUSTICE-INVOLVED

Before 2020, individuals who were justice-involved were stigmatized in the workforce setting, requiring them to check a box to identify as a former offender. Today, this population is regarded as a group of untapped talent eligible for a "second chance" to assimilate into society and obtain a livable wage. This talent pipeline has been a long-standing issue in technical industries, as work in these fields often has shallow talent pools. From an educational and workforce perspective, incarcerated individuals can develop and advance their skill sets through various prison education programs. Most states sponsor programs through their community college systems. Additionally, several not-for-profit agencies in the public and private sectors have developed programs to motivate, elevate, and hire justice-involved individuals.

Impact of Shifting Workforce Demographics on Talent Management

According to Gallup, 2020, and other researchers, each of the demographics identified in this chapter has a unique set of standards that drive their preferences for working conditions. In what follows we will explore key factors such as the work environment, employer brand, technology, advancement opportunities, sustainability, core values, diversity management, leadership style, and culture.

Despite each group's motivation to grow, develop, and compete, fears about how technology will impact their current job status and skills remain a significant concern. According to the World Economic Forum, automation is expected to disrupt one-third of all jobs globally.[21] Technical industries such as manufacturing, construction, and engineering are key drivers of economic growth and competitive advantage. Within the manufacturing sector, the production of electric vehicles, semiconductors, and textiles continues to gain momentum through the application of advanced manufacturing techniques. Within the construction industry, technology is being utilized in various ways, including 3D printing of walls, drones for inspections, and bricklaying. In engineering, new fields are emerging or being elevated, such as mechatronics, cybersecurity, and virtual reality. In 2025, the integration of emerging smart technologies into cars and homes is transforming engineering curricula. As new fields expand, how does outreach to diverse demographics become a key focus for HR practitioners, educators, and policymakers? This question will be explored in Chapters 5 and 6.

Community Colleges' Role in Talent Development

Community colleges serve as the economic engine that fuels the workforce for rural communities. To impact your talent or labor pool in technical industries, connecting with community colleges is key. With approximately 1200 community colleges in the United States, the opportunity to connect with top talent in your state or region is attainable. Every state is grappling with how to attract, recruit, and retain talent in technical industries. If you are an employee seeking to be hired, contact your local community college system or individual community college for assistance. If you have an idea of the type of skills you need, you can contact the college and ask about the programs that align with your preferred skill sets. If no program addresses a majority of your skills, you can potentially work with the college to apply for grants and build a curriculum for your industry's needs. We will share more about this in Chapter 6.

Technology and Talent Management

Digital technologies have heavily impacted recruitment activities within the field. Recruiters have been able to cast a wider net to connect with potential talent pipelines. Recruiters are no longer limited to static candidate engagements, which we refer to as "recruiting by hardscapes." Hardscapes, in landscaping, refer to hard materials such as bricks, pavers, and stones that create a defined path from your house to the pool or garden. In recruiting, these traditional recruiting paths (i.e., newspapers, in-person, and internet job boards) connected people to work when boundaries mattered. Today, talent pipelines do not need to be sourced from a specific geographic location or to conduct work in a precise location. Recruiting through social media, job platforms, networking, and other dynamic strategies provides the most access to a diverse range of candidates. To keep pace with technological advancements, HR practitioners must expand their knowledge of any systems necessary to ensure broader outreach to regions, states, and local communities. For more information on conducting this outreach, refer to Chapters 6 and 7. Furthermore, other evidence-based talent management practices are available to assist HR practitioners with current trends. Consulting firms, such as Gallup and McKinsey, and professional associations, including the Society for Human Resource Management (SHRM) and the Association for Talent Development (ATD), contribute to the field through research, case studies, and frameworks. However, our Talent Expansion Framework (TXF) is beneficial as it addresses both scholarly and practitioner needs, encompassing the components of HR practice, the contributors to the talent development framework, and guiding questions to help facilitate the implementation across your organization.

Adapting Talent Management Strategies

The Fourth Industrial Revolution is constantly perpetuating change. The effective recruiting and retention strategies of the past are no longer effective. Technology is transforming the way we work, and it must also have an impact on how we recruit and retain talent. Within the organizational culture, it is essential for employees to feel valued, from their initial recruitment conversation through to their exit interview. To ensure a sense of belonging across all diverse talent pipelines, we offer the following recommendations to help companies make their culture visible and observable through their external brands (e.g., via staff reviews on Glassdoor and LinkedIn, as well as community recognition).

Automated Applicant Systems and Biased Selection

Although most applicant tracking systems vary, they all share common pitfalls for candidates. A significant barrier to capturing employee skills and experiences is the duplication of questions that occur when candidates have uploaded their résumés to your system. Take time to ensure this phase of your process is streamlined.

Selection bias occurs when specific individuals or groups are systematically excluded, overrepresented, or underrepresented in a dataset or process, resulting in outcomes that do not accurately reflect the broader population. This bias can skew findings, create unfair outcomes, and compromise the validity of decisions or predictions. According to a 2022 roundtable discussion by the Equal Employment Opportunity Commission (EEOC), research exists to substantiate that automated hiring systems can perpetuate inequality by failing to optimize for diverse perspectives.[22] Automated hiring tools have been shown to disadvantage Black candidates and women, often downgrading their applications. Other problems occur when using virtual interviewing tools, which may interfere with or unfairly rate individuals with disabilities based on communication style, behaviors, or tone of assessment.

Collaborative HR Management (Strategic—HR Professionals, Leaders, Supervisors)

By constantly perpetuating change, the Fourth Industrial Revolution requires new skill sets and collaborations. Similarly, the structure of HR needs to change to meet the new demands. Typically, a company, depending on its size, may have an HR manager, an HR generalist, or a talent acquisition specialist (in a department of three or more). However, this approach may be outdated as technology may assist with managing some aspects of the human resource administrative functions. However, the change in authority and oversight will require more strategic leadership engagement. Based on multiple case studies across various industry sizes, additional input is required to ensure a non-biased selection process. Additionally, training is required for both HR management staff and hiring managers. Failure to locate a viable candidate is most often caused by the hiring committee, not a lack of diverse candidates. Based on our experience, HR staff need a set of skills to succeed in this current industrial age. These include skills in data analysis, data management, decision-making, communication, lifelong learning, networking, and either fluency in multiple languages (including American Sign Language [ASL]) or English Language Learners, those who speak other languages and English is not their primary language. To attract, recruit, and retain an inclusive workforce, managers should recognize the significance of language barriers on belonging, confidence, and capability to meet performance goals. By proactively strengthening effective communication skills of English Language Learners (ELL), mutual engagement and productivity can be achieved.

Internal Communication Strategies

Effective internal communication requires a deliberate, top-down strategy that emphasizes transparency, consistency, and timely messaging from leadership. Clear and frequent communication between management and team members fosters trust and alignment, particularly during periods of change or growth. Leveraging diverse communication styles, formats, and technologies, such as real-time messaging, video updates, and collaborative platforms, can enhance engagement, support training, and strengthen cross-functional collaboration in technical environments. In Chapter 6, we will address forms of communication that occur at the strategic level and how communication styles immediately impact the recruitment and retention of all populations regardless of race, gender, socioeconomic status, ethnicity, or citizenship.

Prioritize Branding

Understanding the candidate's perspective on your organization is crucial for employers. Just as you need to conduct outreach and awareness to reach potential applicants, applicants need to understand how to reach you. Within technical industries, many firms are small businesses. Of those small businesses, less than one-third have a website. Websites of those that do may not be as accessible or user-friendly and may lack universal design principles for those with disabilities. Although budget is a factor in enhancing processes, visibility, and likability, the employees represent the first brand ambassadors. They should want to share the best places to work on social media, recruiting platforms (i.e., Glassdoor), and other channels.

Future Challenges for HR Professionals in Managing a Diverse Workforce

HR professionals must continue to upskill to meet the changing technological trends. New technologies, such as recruitment tools and AI, as well as managing ethical issues, remain a priority. Therefore, individuals considering a career in HR should engage in lifelong learning and actively create opportunities to contribute to their communities. Other opportunities and specific recommendations for leadership courses, programs, and building brand awareness will be addressed in Chapters 6 and 7.

Preparing for Diverse Talent Management

The business case for diversity became popular in the 1990s.[23] Ultimately, managing diversity was recognized as a required practice for ensuring more substantial business performance results. Many HR practitioners have scrambled to take additional training on effective strategies to attract, recruit, and retain diverse talent. While the exact strategy applies across industries, the characteristics of talent working in technical industries require a unique approach. Employers face challenges in overcoming the industries' reputation, including perceptions of positions as dangerous, dirty, low-paying, and unskilled. Additionally, age and gender are factors in recruiting potential candidates into the workforce.

As the technical industries become increasingly global, customer supply chains and industry clients must prioritize racial and cultural diversity. To ensure that a homogeneous workforce does not hinder current technical fields, HR managers must take action to attract, retain, and recruit diverse talent across all levels of the business hierarchy.

Building the business case for diversity essentially means ensuring that all stakeholders involved in the business (staff, leaders, customers, and competitors) provide credibility and validity to the argument that diversity strengthens innovation, productivity, and performance. Are you prepared to navigate talent in the future of work? What is your talent acquisition (recruitment process), and what modifications are needed? How will diversity management factor in that change? As a broad, informal evaluation, we recommend considering the value, evidence, and reinforcement of diversity within your organization. Thinking about your current diversity management goals, are they observable, achievable, reinforceable, and sustainable? Consider the following illustration in your work setting.

As researchers and scholar-practitioners, we research to test our hypotheses or theories. During a site visit, we aim to corroborate the data collected during the interview process. During this process, we take field notes to support or oppose the case study or question, thereby backing up our qualitative data. In the case of diversity management, we provide the following examples from the "field" as a visual presence of diversity management practices in industry:

1. **Observable:** Describe the visible aspects of the environment that indicate racially, ethnically, and culturally diverse locations. Here are some attributes we noted:

   a. Main visitors' area: appropriate signage in various languages, signs that explicitly state all people are welcome.
   b. Mission, vision, and core values in multiple areas of the factory floor, with multiple languages.
   c. Is there diverse representation among the leadership and staff?
   d. Are there indications for collaborative learning environments (i.e., co-working with robots, diverse teams)?
   e. What barriers are hindering a diversified, collaborative working environment?
   f. Are you in an urban, rural, or metro community?
   g. Is your general population diverse?
   h. If you don't have access to a diverse talent pool, how can you attract top talent?

2. **Achievable:** How are career advancement and promotion activities equitably shared, delivered, and obtained?
    a. Skills Matrix, list of productivity and goals shared across organizations where leaders and staff can chart their personal growth.
    b. Is there accountability in leadership and staff to work among themselves to track progress?
    c. Who is responsible for ensuring new training opportunities are explored and accessible (i.e. AI courses, cybersecurity)?
3. Reinforceable: Who or what needs to change perspective or leave the organization?
    a. Leaders
    b. Employees
    c. Customers
    d. Community
    e. Industry perspective shift
4. **Sustainable:** How can you retain a diverse workforce?

The example above serves as a starting point for discussion within your organization. More importantly, how would this exercise look if future applicants visited your factory, facility, or job site? Would there be evidence of who you are as an employer?

Work-Life Balance

Within manufacturing, prioritizing work-life balance may involve offering flexible scheduling options, such as job rotation, shift overlaps, early departure, transportation, childcare, and other benefits. However, technical industries may face the biggest challenges in accommodating these schedules. As noted previously, the use of technologies to offer flexible scheduling has been explored in construction, notably through Building Information Modeling (BIM). We will explore other opportunities to create this flexibility in Chapters 3 and 9.

Building an Innovative Workforce

Building a future-ready workforce entails attracting and recruiting new talent, developing existing employees through training initiatives, and reconfiguring work processes to address any mismatches between job requirements and employee skills. According to a 2024 report by McKinsey entitled "A New Future of Work: The Race to Deploy AI and Raise Skills in

Europe and Beyond," 30 percent of hours worked could be automated by 2030.[24] As researchers and practitioners in learning and development, we offer the following tips for engaging innovation across technical industries, which will be expanded upon across the topic-specific areas throughout the text. As such, the action steps listed below will be further explained or isolated as unique leadership strategies to ensure competitive advantage.

HR Action Step: Assess Workforce Development Needs (Gap Analysis)

Determine the current state of the workforce within your county/city, state, and region. Do not leave this to other experts (i.e., economic development experts, workforce boards) to do on their own. Conduct your own research and determine your employer's needs. Next, consult with your city, county, and data leads to identify opportunities for your organization to address gaps. In our research and experience, we have observed that city programs often partner with community colleges to offer introductory courses to the broader community, serving as a precursor to a new career. This primer course sets the tone for connecting incumbent workers, students, and career transitioners to technical industries. States with robust workforce programs, such as California, Ohio, Maryland, North Carolina, and Washington, have served as models for integrating cutting-edge, innovative tools, programs, and technologies into their technical education programs.

HR Action Step: Awareness of Employer High-Demand Skills

Conduct direct conversations with employers using survey tools, focus groups, live convenings, hosted listening sessions, and employer panels to identify specific needs, from entry-level to senior leadership. Monitor ongoing workforce trends and adjust accordingly to stay competitive across various industries. By understanding the skills required by employers, known as benchmarking, you can stay up to date on your individual and organizational skills.

HR Action Step: Leadership Development Training

As technological changes occur, taking inventory of your leadership skills will be critical for top-, mid-, and entry-level leaders. Staying up to date on talent management language, strategies, and tools is essential if you are to provide collaborative leadership and drive success across the organization. For more information, refer to Chapter 4.

HR Action Step: Integrate Digital Recruitment Tools

Immersion in new recruitment tools will enable powerful, real-time interactions with candidates and applicant tracking systems. Possibilities for identifying the latest tools include participating in association meetings, networking, and attending vendor demonstrations to support the implementation of tools in the recruitment and retention process. When tools can enhance candidate performance, the quality of recruitment and retention improves.

HR Action Step: Embrace Data Analytics and Artificial Intelligence (AI)

Determine the source of data/statistics and outcomes. Are you accessing data from reputable sources, such as the American Survey (US Census), Bureau of Labor Statistics, ONET, and technical associations (the Society for Human Resource Management [SHRM], manufacturing institutes, construction, etc.)? Is this data reputable, transferable, and applicable to your specific organization?

HR Action Step: Foster a Learning Culture

Adopting a learning culture that fosters consistent opportunities for advancement will strengthen the talent pool. Consider key possibilities for implementing short bursts of learning through micro-credentialing, LinkedIn learning, on-the-job training, and cooperative learning. Incorporating short- and long-term training into the organizational culture will ensure that all staff members have equal access to learning opportunities and a clear career path for advancement within the organization. Within technical industries, competency- and skill-based programs exist to address industry needs. These industry-based competencies and resources on competency-based education networks will be explored in Chapter 8.

Conclusion

HR practitioners, policymakers, and other community partners must maintain a firm grasp on the evolving skills, technologies, and AI models that are transforming the way we work. To accomplish this, HR practitioners need to consider their own individual learning needs, as well as changes to the organizational mission and vision, policies, and political impacts. Additionally, this will significantly impact how the future workforce adapts to these changes, with implications for either exacerbating talent shortages in technical industries or creating opportunities to expand upon them.

Putting It into Practice

This chapter sets the tone for how technology is shaping the landscape of technical industries and provides examples of how HR professionals should engage in professional development and organizational growth. The following are three key areas for HR professionals to consider and expand upon when navigating talent management and technology advancement in technical industries:

1. **Perform Comprehensive Gap Analysis:** Conduct an external (industry-wide) and internal (organizational and individual professional) skills assessment.
2. **Build Technology Skills:** Consistently research and adopt current technologies in HR, and in the technical industry you may be actively working in.
3. **Establish Continuous Outreach and Recruitment:** Exhaust all possibilities for connecting with new talent, developing your existing talent, or recruiting talent from adjacent fields.

Notes

1 U.S. Department of Labor (n.d.). Workforce Development Solutions. https://www.dol.gov/agencies/eta/employers/workforce-development-solutions
2 Groumpos, P. (2021). A Critical Historical and Scientific Overview of all Industrial Revolutions. *IFAC-PapersOnLine*, 54, 464–471. 10.1016/j.ifacol.2021.10.492
3 Cai, L., Ji, Y., Wijekoon, C., Yuan, Y. (2023). Decision-Making on Selection of Talent Management Methods in the Era of Digitalization. *Systems*, *11*(9), 450. https://doi.org/10.3390/systems11109450
4 PwC (2017). Retrieved from https://www.bbc.com/news/business-44849492
5 Ozkazanc-Pan, B. (2019). Diversity and Future of Work: Inequality Abound or Opportunities for All? *Management Decision*, *59*(11), 2645–2659. https://doi.org/10.1108/md-02-2019-0244
6 Bureau of Labor Statistics (2021). Retrieved from: https://www.bls.gov/cps/cpsaat18.htm
7 Kuzior, A., Kettler, K., and Rąb, Ł. (2022). Great Resignation—Ethical, Cultural, Relational, and Personal Dimensions of Generation Y and Z Employees' Engagement. *Sustainability*, *14*(11), 6764. https://doi.org/10.3390/su14116764
8 Calzavara, M., Battini, D., Bogataj, D., Sgarbossa, F., and Zennaro, I. (2019). Ageing Workforce Management in Manufacturing Systems: State of the Art and Future Research Agenda. *International Journal of Production Research*, *58*(3), 729–747. https://doi.org/10.1080/00207543.2019.1600759

9 U.S. Equal Employment Opportunity Commission (2025). Retrieved from https://www.eeoc.gov/2024-annual-performance-report

10 Pew Research Center (2018). Women and Men in STEM Often at Odds Over Workplace Equity. Retrieved from: https://www.pewresearch.org/social-trends/2018/01/09/women-and-men-in-stem-often-at-odds-over-workplace-equity/

11 National Center for Science and Engineering Statistics (NCSES) (2021). *Women, Minorities, and Persons with Disabilities in Science and Engineering: 2021* (NSF 21–321). National Science Foundation. https://ncses.nsf.gov/pubs/wmpd

12 Bahn, K., and Cumming, C. S. (2020, July). Four Graphs on U.S. Occupational Segregation by Race, Ethnicity, Gender. Washington Center for Equitable Growth. https://equitablegrowth.org/four-graphs-on-u-s-occupational-segregation-by-race-ethnicity-and-gender/

13 Santamaría Graff, C. C. (2017). "Build That Wall!": Manufacturing the Enemy, Yet Again. *International Journal of Qualitative Studies in Education*, *30*(10), 999–1005. https://doi.org/10.1080/09518398.2017.1312592

14 Duval-Couetil, N., and Mikulecky, L. (2011). Immigrants, English, and the Workplace. *Journal of Workplace Learning*, *23*(3), 209–223. https://doi.org/10.1108/13665621111117233

15 Moutray, C. (2022, November). Closing the Gender Gap: Recruiting and Retaining Women in Manufacturing. The Manufacturing Institute.

16 Nisha a, R., Subramani, A. K., and Harini, S. (2025). The Role of Human Resources in Creating Gender Equity in an Organization. In H. C. Chandan (ed.), *Enhancing Workplace Productivity Through Gender Equity and Intergenerational Communication*, IGI Global. 10.4018/979-8-3373-2903-1.ch001.

17 Disability Rights North Carolina (n.d.). Retrieved from https://disabilityrightsnc.org

18 Goodwill (n.d.). Retrieved from https://www.goodwill.org

19 Excellence Training Center at Youngstown University (n.d.). Retrieved from https://ysu.edu/excellence-training-center

20 Office of Disability Employment Policy (n.d.). Retrieved from https://www.dol.gov/agencies/odep

21 Alam, S., and Dhamija, P. (2022). Human Resource Development 4.0 (HRD 4.0) in the Apparel Industry of Bangladesh: A Theoretical Framework and Future Research Directions. *International Journal of Manpower*, *43*(2), 263–285. https://doi.org/10.1108/ijm-06-2021-0372

22 U.S. Equal Employment Opportunity Commission (n.d.). EEOC History: 2020–2024. https://www.eeoc.gov/history/eeoc-history-2020-2024#:~:text=The%20EEOC%20and%20OFCCP%20held,of%20automated%20technology%20systems%20in

23 Cox, T. H., and Blake, S. (1991). Managing Cultural Diversity: Implications for Organizational Competitiveness. *The Executive*, *5*(3), 45–56. http://www.jstor.org/stable/4165021

24 McKinsey Global Institute (2024). A New Future of Work: The Race to Deploy AI and Raise Skills in Europe and Beyond. https://www.consultia.co/a-new-future-of-work-the-race-to-deploy-ai-and-raise-skills-in-europe-and-beyond/

Chapter 3

Building on Origins of Talent Opportunity

Disclaimer: Due to recent policy shifts related to affirmative action and workplace inclusion efforts, modifications were made to this chapter to ensure alignment with current guidance. The context and practices discussed remain relevant to strengthening national talent pipelines and addressing persistent workforce shortages. This topic has reshaped occupational roles, introduced new career pathways, and influenced long-standing professionals working within talent development and organizational culture improvement. We do not position ourselves as legal experts in affirmative action. However, an overview of affirmative action is essential as a factual foundation for understanding historical approaches to expanding access to opportunity and workforce participation. Readers who wish to deepen their knowledge are encouraged to explore insights from leading contributors in this field. We also consulted a subject matter expert in affirmative action, whose reflections informed the practical considerations included here for industries such as manufacturing, engineering, and construction. As political landscapes evolve, terminology, expectations, and frameworks will likely continue to shift. What remains consistent is the importance of developing strategies that support attraction, preparation, and retention across a broad range of potential workers. For this reason, returning to the original intent of affirmative action offers clarity; its purpose was to expand pathways into employment and strengthen equitable access to opportunity. Regardless of future terminology changes, the central question is not what we call these efforts, but how we continue to design workforce strategies that mobilize a diverse range of talent required for the future of work. As researchers and practitioners, we state the facts and provide our opinions where appropriate. The content is meant to provide background historical context for your interpretation and implementation that best suits your organization.

DOI: 10.4324/9781003515937-4

Advancing Talent Acquisition and Capacity

This chapter introduces the historical foundations that influenced access to employment opportunities and then transitions into broader talent acquisition strategies that support employer workforce needs. The emphasis here is not on terminology or political language, but rather on strengthening workforce capacity across sectors and preparing organizations for rapid technological change. Technical industries play a vital role in regional and national economic growth. Expanding the available talent pool within these sectors is essential for sustaining productivity, supporting job quality, and enabling upward mobility across communities. A workforce that draws from a wide range of skill backgrounds and career pathways is better positioned to meet emerging demands, spark innovation, and maintain competitive advantage in the 21st-century economy.

We invite readers to consider this book as a Talent Expansion Guide, one that supports a shared vision for shaping, developing, and advancing the future workforce. It is intended to amplify pathways into technical careers, support skill development at scale, and position organizations to adapt and thrive as work continues to evolve.

Affirmative Action: Executive Orders

In the 1960s, President John F. Kennedy enacted affirmative action through Executive Order 10925 to ensure equal treatment of job applicants regardless of race, color, religion, sex, or national origin. According to the American Bar Association, an executive order is a "signed, written, and published directive from the President of the United States that manages federal government operations."[1] Various types of executive orders exist. Policies address education, civil rights, and the environment. Although executive orders enable swift action on policies, legal safeguards and checks ensure that the balance is maintained across the government.

Some prominent examples of executive orders that have impacted on civil rights include:

1. **Executive Order 8802:** Issued in 1941 by President Franklin D. Roosevelt, it prohibited racial discrimination in the defense industry and led to the establishment of the Fair Employment Practices Committee.
2. **Executive Order 9981:** Issued in 1948 by President Harry S. Truman, desegregated the armed forces, marking a significant step toward civil rights reforms.
3. **Executive Order 13228:** Issued in 2001 by President George W. Bush, it established the Office of Homeland Security in response to the 9/11 terrorist attacks.

There are specific executive orders that require government contractors to comply with affirmative action. These orders are responsible for guiding government contractors in conducting business with the US government. These orders enforce key requirements that, if not followed, create legal barriers for contractors and disrupt their access to funding, including grants, contract awards, and operational support. Compliance with these government standards has historically only impacted federal businesses. If you have not been part of the federal contracting space in human resources, these requirements, protocols, and processes may be new to you. However, they can act as levers to ensure equality, equity, and fairness across industries.

First, we will provide an overview of relevant executive orders and then offer comparable strategies aligned with the former approach to attract diverse talent. Finally, we will share valuable "from the field" practitioner illustrations and observations to help you implement affirmative action planning successfully. Due to the legal, ethical, and compliance nature of this work, the specificity, intentionality, and organization of attracting, recruiting, and retaining talent remain critical in the federal market. Still, it has implications for strengthening diverse talent in all sectors and markets (federal, private, and nonprofit).

The Federal Acquisition Regulation (FAR) regulates affirmative action requirements, which are driven by Executive Order 11246,[2] the Rehabilitation Act of 1973,[3] and the Vietnam Era Veterans' Readjustment Assistance Act (VEVRAA).[4] These combined layers align to guide the C-suite and leaders on recruitment processes.

Executive Order 11246

Coverage: Applies to federal contractors and subcontractors with contracts exceeding $10,000.

Requirements: Contractors must not discriminate based on race, color, religion, sex, sexual orientation, gender identity, or national origin. They are also required to take affirmative action to ensure equal employment opportunities.

Affirmative Action Plan (AAP): Contractors with 50 or more employees and a contract of $50,000 or more must develop and maintain a written AAP. This plan includes analyzing workforce composition, identifying problem areas, and specific action-oriented programs to address the underrepresentation of minorities and women.

Executive Order 11246, signed by President Lyndon Johnson on September 24, 1965, established requirements for non-discriminatory practices in hiring and employment on the part of US government contractors. It prohibits federal contractors and federally assisted construction contractors and subcontractors who do business with the federal government from discriminating in employment decisions based on race, color, religion, sex, or national origin. It also requires contractors to take affirmative action to ensure that applicants are employed and that employees are treated during employment without regard to their race, color, religion, sex, or national origin.

Today, Executive Order 11246, as amended, has been further strengthened over the years. It remains a significant safeguard, protecting the rights of workers employed by federal contractors—which includes approximately one-fifth of the US labor force—to remain free from discrimination based on their race, color, religion, sex, sexual orientation, gender identity, or national origin, and opens the doors of opportunity through its affirmative action provisions.

The Rehabilitation Act of 1973 (Section 503)

Coverage: Applies to federal contractors and subcontractors with contracts exceeding $15,000.

Requirements: Contractors must take affirmative action to employ and advance in employment qualified individuals with disabilities.

AAP: Contractors with 50 or more employees and a contract of $50,000 or more must prepare and maintain a written AAP for individuals with disabilities.

Vietnam Era Veterans' Readjustment Assistance Act (VEVRAA)

Coverage: Applies to federal contractors and subcontractors with contracts of $150,000 or more.

Requirements: Contractors must take affirmative action to employ and advance in employment qualified protected veterans.

AAP: Contractors with 50 or more employees and a contract of $150,000 or more must develop and maintain a written AAP for veterans.

Enforcement of Affirmative Action Requirements

The Office of Federal Contract Compliance Programs (OFCCP), part of the US Department of Labor, enforces affirmative action requirements for federal contractors. The enforcement mechanisms include compliance review, assistance, investigations, and enforcement actions. Traditionally, the OFCCP can conduct compliance reviews of federal contractors to ensure adherence to affirmative action requirements. These reviews may occur in person or through a formal administrative exchange with HR professionals and the OFCCP. Examples include desk audits, onsite reviews, and offsite analysis. The OFCCP provides technical assistance through shared resources, training, and documentation to help contractors and HR professionals understand and comply with affirmative action requirements. Despite their assistance, the authors offer several tips from the field in this section.

Although the OFCCP may occur regularly or as part of a random audit, strict protocols must be observed during the visit. Typically, the contractor will receive notification of a pending visit and can take time to review their compliance issues. However, in the event of compliance issues, the contractor will be given time to resolve infractions. If a contractor is cited for non-compliance, the OFCCP can escalate enforcement actions. These can include requiring the contractor to take corrective measures, entering into conciliation agreements, or imposing sanctions such as withholding contract payments, canceling contracts, or debarment from future contracts.

Affirmative Action Planning Experience

> Case Study—My Personal Story (Dr. Suber): *The year was 2006, and my husband had recently opened a new construction firm. With two kids under five and one on the way, I was learning to build, develop, and implement a small business HR department from scratch—a Department of One. In addition to navigating the new hiring and retention requirements, the compliance requirements involved in government contracting were critically important, as I did not want to wait for my learning curve to catch up, which actively caused delays in my ability to build our construction workforce. How did I begin the informal learning process of creating an Affirmative Action Plan and hiring? I started by understanding the plan's components, who would be responsible and accountable for ensuring it was maintained (me), and that all staff were aware of the plan, its content, and their responsibility for representing it.*

While it was a compliance issue back then and remains a federal requirement, this best practice can be carried out regularly, keeping you intentional, focused, and prepared. Next, the importance of a strategic and non-compliance-based approach will be addressed. However, the steps below can serve as a starting point to facilitate your strides for inclusive HR hiring. These recommendations, lessons learned, and tips are based on experiential learning and practical application. We did not expand upon any theory of HR frameworks to address this AAP focus area but drew on best practices to establish a foundation for recruitment.

Beyond Affirmative Action: The Current Context

In the wake of recent legal and political shifts that have curtailed or redefined affirmative action, organizations and educators face renewed pressure to articulate why diversity, equity, and inclusion remain essential—not as mandates, but as markers of excellence and innovation. While some interpret this era as a retreat from prior diversity efforts, it is better understood as an invitation to reaffirm the intrinsic value of varied identities, perspectives, and lived experiences in the workplace. In today's complex global economy, success depends on collective intelligence, on teams that bring together different ways of seeing, solving, and leading. Diversity of thought and background enhances problem-solving, mitigates bias, and drives organizational adaptability. The current moment, therefore, calls not for silence or avoidance, but for intentional, evidence-based strategies that sustain pluralism and belonging beyond compliance frameworks.

Authors' Tip #1

Reframe the narrative from fulfilling diversity mandates to cultivating organizational excellence through inclusion. Diversity should be presented not as a legal requirement but as a source of innovation, adaptability, and collective strength in the workplace.

Authors' Tip #2

Use language that emphasizes belonging and excellence. Terms such as *inclusive excellence*, *collaborative advantage*, and *diversity of thought* can help position diversity efforts as core to strategic success rather than peripheral compliance.

Authors' Tip #3

Ground your arguments in evidence. Reference research demonstrates that diverse teams outperform homogeneous ones in problem-solving, creativity, and decision-making.[5]

Authors' Tip #4

Acknowledge the evolving policy context. Briefly address recent changes to affirmative action policies, then pivot to constructive solutions—such as holistic recruitment, mentorship development, and equity-minded leadership practices.

Authors' Tip #5

Highlight actionable pathways. Provide real-world examples of organizations fostering inclusion through transparent advancement processes, bias interruption initiatives, and intentional culture building.

Authors' Tip #6

Invite reflection and accountability. Encourage readers to consider how their institutions can uphold fairness, access, and respect for different principles that remain vital regardless of shifting political climates.

HR Action Step: Build on Lessons from Past Workforce Planning Models

A strong talent pipeline begins with structure and intentionality. Many organizations historically used Affirmative Action Plans or similar frameworks to organize workforce data and hiring goals. Those same planning principles (clarity, consistency, and accountability) remain essential today. Developing a centralized workforce plan or "talent blueprint" helps organizations track recruitment strategies, training initiatives, and advancement pathways. Whether digital or in print, the plan should be accessible to all decision-makers and evolve as market demands shift. The aim is to position workforce planning as an ongoing process of growth and renewal rather than a static compliance activity.

HR Action Step: Define Talent Goals Around Organizational Strengths and Future Needs

Modern talent strategies should focus on aligning recruitment goals with business priorities. Instead of viewing hiring through the lens of filling quotas, leaders can define success by the organization's ability to attract and retain individuals with the skills, mindsets, and experiences needed for long-term sustainability. Setting clear, measurable goals, such as increasing early career pipelines, strengthening technical competencies, or enhancing leadership readiness, ensures that recruitment contributes directly to organizational growth. Goals tied to mission and innovation inspire momentum and buy-in across all levels of leadership.

HR Action Step: Use National and Industry Resources to Strengthen Workforce Systems

Federal, state, and industry organizations offer valuable data, tools, and resources that can help businesses with benchmark progress and refine workforce planning. Agencies like the Department of Labor and sector-based councils publish workforce projections, skills frameworks, and best-practice models for recruitment and retention. Small and mid-sized organizations, in particular, can benefit from adopting these resources to build scalable systems that support talent development and mobility.

Best practices include:

- **Assessing Workforce Needs: Analyze current and projected skill gaps to guide recruitment and training priorities.**
- Maintaining Transparent Processes: Document key recruitment and promotion decisions to inform future planning, as forecasting will ensure knowledge management continuity should a leadership transition occur.
- Leveraging Tools and Templates: Use available workforce planning templates and metrics dashboards to measure outcomes and ensure continuous improvement.
- Communicating Vision and Value: Signal commitment to growth and opportunity through clear messaging in job postings and internal communications to ensure candidates know your brand.

HR Action Step: Develop Data-Informed Talent Strategies

Effective workforce development depends on meaningful data. HR leaders should collect and analyze information related to recruitment sources, retention rates, internal promotions, and turnover patterns. This data can reveal where pipelines are strong and where additional investment is needed. Tracking metrics such as time-to-fill, training participation, and leadership readiness enables organizations to anticipate future needs and adjust accordingly. Data turns intuition into strategy, helping companies design proactive approaches to succession planning, skill development, and workforce agility.

HR Action Step: Invest in Leadership Development and Continuous Learning

Sustainable pipelines depend on leaders who understand how to nurture talent. Training supervisors and managers to identify potential, coach employees, and create growth opportunities is key to long-term success. Leadership development should not be reserved for executives; it should be embedded at every level of the organization. When leaders model curiosity, mentorship, and collaboration, they foster a workplace culture that attracts high-performing professionals and encourages them to stay. Even in smaller organizations, investing in targeted professional development, such as onboarding programs, mentoring networks, and skill academies, creates pathways that strengthen retention and promote advancement from within.

Building a strong talent pipeline is less about compliance and more about cultivation. Organizations that plan intentionally, measure progress, and invest in people will be best positioned to meet future challenges. The goal is not merely to hire but to develop, empower, and sustain a workforce that grows with the organization. Through structured planning, data-informed decision-making, and leadership commitment, companies can create thriving ecosystems where talent is continuously discovered, developed, and advanced.

EEOC Resolution Related to Racial Discrimination

In 2023, the Chicago Meat Authority, a meat-processing company, paid $1.1 million to resolve a discrimination case involving a Black employee who encountered racial harassment and retaliation. Additionally, the company was found to have unfairly excluded Black applicants during the hiring process. A consent decree serves as a legally binding performance improvement plan, enforceable by a court, to which each party agrees. The decree set forth the following actions:

- **Hiring of Rejected Applicants:** Black applicants who were previously denied employment would be given opportunities to work at the facility.
- **Efforts to Improve Hiring Practices:** The company agreed to make good-faith efforts to increase the hiring of Black employees.
- **Anti-harassment Training and Policies:** Mandatory training and policies to prevent future harassment and discrimination.

Although the Equal Employment Opportunity Commission (EEOC) investigation and subsequent ruling pertain to a private company, all companies need to understand the consequences of failing to meet their diverse hiring obligations. In this regard, affirmative action planning should not only be undertaken to mitigate legal action but also to ensure compliance. Affirmative action planning can be used as a lever to inform, guide, and monitor recruitment processes and procedures. We acknowledge that examining the original intent behind affirmative action may have had a "quota-based" intent, which is insufficient to achieve diversity. However,

SME Reflection: Affirmative Action Plans

Since 1980, John DiDio, the former director of a local Virginia area office of the EEOC, has developed and monitored Affirmative Action Plans, including those with charges of employment discrimination. The italicized quotes from him below offer vital insights into how Affirmative Action Plans inform government audits and evaluations, as well as the benefits they provide employers in diversifying their recruitment efforts.

Guide Recruitment Practices

Research suggests that small and medium-sized businesses conduct recruitment on an ad hoc and informal basis.* John's experiences validate this finding: *"Institutions that don't have this federal requirement may . . . make the recruitment effort in a very haphazard manner."*

Affirmative Action Plans differ depending on the type of industry (construction, engineering, or manufacturing). Despite their differences, John says Affirmative Action Plans *"provide the structure and methodology . . . on how to do their recruitment process in a more fair, objective, and organized manner."*

Monitor Recruitment Efforts

Affirmative Action Plans enable employers to monitor and enhance diverse recruitment practices. For example, employers can adjust their recruitment approach by evaluating recruitment efforts on a quarterly, semi-annual, or annual basis. *"If they find out that their applicant pool is not as diverse as they want it to be, then, in fact, they can modify, add, or subtract the way they recruit."*

Outreach to Underrepresented Populations

Affirmative Action Plan questions have evolved through the development of executive orders, enabling employers to *"reach underrepresented areas that were not fully in the workforce."*

AAPs reveal employers *"have set up different training programs [e.g., apprenticeships] and other opportunities to go into the high schools to share with students. That [outreach] covers all types of racial, . . . sex, male and female. The goal not quota in the 1980s for females in construction was 6.9% within trades. That goal has not changed; it is still challenging to find qualified females to do some of the particular tasks, and it's for many reasons.*" However, Di Dio says, "*There has been an increase in many minority groups in particular jobs.*" The goal for females in trades remains at 6.9 percent today.

* Barrett, R., and Mayson, S. (2007). Human Resource Management in Growing Small Firms. *Journal of Small Business and Enterprise Development, 14*(2), 307–320.

going beyond "affirmative action" and leaning into the affirmative action planning protocols can offer a proactive, practical approach to strengthening diversity in technical industries.

Inclusive Terms Defined

Since the mid-20th century, terminology related to diversity and opportunity has evolved alongside changes in public policy, workforce needs, and institutional practice. Early discussions of diversity were closely tied to affirmative action initiatives beginning in the 1960s. Over time, additional concepts and frameworks emerged to address access, participation, and organizational effectiveness across educational and employment contexts. In this section, we define and distinguish key terms commonly referenced in contemporary discussions of diversity, equity, and inclusion (DEI). The goal is to clarify how these terms have been used historically and how they are currently understood across higher education, business, and workforce development settings. Clear definitions are essential for productive dialogue, effective leadership, and informed decision-making, particularly during periods of policy transition. Recent changes in state and institutional policy have altered how DEI-related work is structured and labeled within higher education and some industry contexts. These shifts have implications for organizational roles, talent pipelines, and workforce capacity, which are explored in greater depth in Chapter 11. Here, we focus on establishing a shared language to support readers' understanding of the concepts that continue to shape workforce systems, institutional practices, and leadership strategies across sectors.

Diversity-Defined

When we conducted a manual search for the definition of "diversity," it was not easy to find definitions that did not include complementary words like "inclusion" and "equality." We searched AI and academic journals and found an infinite number of definitions of diversity. We put in the prompt, "*What is the most common definition of diversity used in most organizations?*" diversity refers to the presence of differences among people in a workplace or group, particularly in terms of characteristics such as race, ethnicity, gender, age, sexual orientation, disability, religion, socioeconomic status, and cultural background. In addition to this common definition, we offer four main definitions based on HR-related practitioner sources and educational and governmental sources. These definitions were selected to broadly address the implications of diversity in business, education, and policy.

Diversity: Business-Related Definition

In McKinsey's report "What Is Diversity, Equity, and Inclusion?"[6] from 2022, diversity is defined as a broad term addressing "who is represented in the workplace." More specifically, they address different forms of representation, including gender, age, ethnicity, physical ability, and neurodiversity:

> *Definition: The inclusion of people with different backgrounds, experiences, and perspectives in the workplace.*

Diversity: Higher Education-Related Definition

Within education, it was helpful to capture the broad, institutional definition based on the American Council of Education (ACE) and the Association for the Study of Higher Education (ASHE). It was also important to emphasize that, within higher education, most publicly funded colleges in the 2023/24 academic year included the word "diversity" in their school strategic plans. *We highlighted a few below. However, these examples are either no longer valid or acceptable, given the new political developments that occurred during the book's drafting. We chose to keep them in the chapter to provide a historical context for the language before the requirement to remove references to DEI.*

COLLEGE-SPECIFIC DEFINITIONS

According to Penn State University[7] diversity refers to *the numerical representation of faculty, staff, and students with different social identities, backgrounds, and experiences.*

According to the University of Michigan[8] diversity is *expressed in myriad forms, including race and ethnicity, gender and gender identity, sexual orientation, socioeconomic status, language, culture, national origin, religious commitments, age, (dis)ability status, and political perspective.*

Diversity: Government/Policy-Related Definition

The following governmental definition of diversity comes from the US Department of Education/Office of Inspector General's Diversity, Equity, Inclusion, and Accessibility Strategic Plan for Fiscal Years 2023–2028:

> *Definition: Diversity is a collection of individual attributes that help agencies pursue organizational objectives efficiently and effectively.*[9]

Equity-Defined

According to *Merriam-Webster's Dictionary*, equity is *"freedom from bias or favoritism."*

Equity: Education-Related Definition

The Colorado Department of Higher Education[10] defines "equity" as *intentionally removing structural barriers and providing all students with the specific support they need to succeed.*

Equity: Government-Related Definition

Several government-based definitions exist for the word "equity." However, it is notable that others have been officially deleted from websites while this book was being edited.

Inclusion-Defined

According to ChatGPT, using the prompt, *"What is the most common definition of inclusion used in most organizations?"* inclusion refers to the intentional effort to create an environment where individuals of all backgrounds, identities, and perspectives feel valued, respected, and able to contribute fully to the organization's success. According to Deloitte's report "Unleashing the Power of Inclusion, Attracting and Engaging the Evolving Workforce,"[11] 80 percent of respondents consider inclusion important when choosing an employer. Before all the reversals of DEI, many organizations had separate definitions, with many government organizations adopting the version issued through executive order, as noted below.

Inclusion: Government-Related Definition

Executive Order 14035, signed by President Joseph R. Biden, defined inclusion as *"the recognition, appreciation, and use of the talents and skills of employees of all backgrounds."*[12]

Instead of providing examples of inclusion as we did for diversity and equity, we prefer to highlight that inclusivity and inclusion seem to have more staying power than all the other words in DEI.

In the remaining section, we will dive deeper into the challenges and setbacks of DEI within higher education and business settings. We will provide examples of companies and organizations that continue to model and support effective, intentional strategies for attracting, recruiting, and retaining diverse talent. Finally, we will discuss ways upcoming chapters will address future workforce needs.

DEI Has Fallen in Higher Education

Diversity, equity, and inclusion as a recruitment form and cultural and social construction have fallen. How will the policy changes in the DEI space impact on our definition of diversity-, equity-, and inclusion-based practices? Some universities have begun rebranding their offices nationwide to distance themselves from their association with DEI. There are a few examples below, but there will be many more transitions and traversing of language. We find this noteworthy as universities will continue to struggle to comply with the laws while supporting students, faculty, and staff:

- University of South Carolina changed the name of its Office of Diversity, Equity, and Inclusion to the "Division of Access, Civil Rights, and Community Engagement."
- Clemson University similarly renamed its former DEI office the "Division of Community Engagement."

As public higher education systems and states revise policies that restrict the use of certain workplace value statements, how will institutions and employers continue to demonstrate accountability for expanding talent pipelines and attracting a broad range of qualified candidates?

Ripple Effects of Talent Investment Strategies on Business Outcomes

Prior to recent administrative changes, many major organizations had been expanding initiatives focused on building stronger talent pipelines, strengthening inclusive workplace climates, and improving workforce engagement. We identified several examples for your review based on publicly available documentation and organizational reporting. We recommend monitoring how these companies adjust and recalibrate these strategies moving forward, as evolving policy shifts will likely influence how firms communicate, align, and resource these approaches over time.

Business Rankings, Talent Development, and Workforce Pipelines—Large to Small (Engineering, Construction, Manufacturing)

Several large consulting firms (such as Korn Ferry, McKinsey, and Deloitte) have published business rankings that assess how organizations strengthen workforce capacity, culture, and human capital strategies. In addition, within construction, engineering, and manufacturing, significant guidance comes from national trade associations and industry sector organizations. These groups were selected based on their historical investment in technical workforce development, funding contributions to the field, and influence in shaping national conversations around talent preparation and productivity.

These associations offer resources to strengthen employer knowledge, expand access to evidence-based workforce development tools, and connect industry to research that supports stronger and more sustainable talent pipelines. Their work goes beyond regulatory compliance and reflects intentional efforts to build high-performing workforces positioned for innovation, resilience, and competitive advantage. Strengthening talent pipelines in construction, engineering, and manufacturing ensures organizations are better prepared for automation, technical transformation, and future workplace demands.

Below, we highlight membership organizations and professional associations that align closely with technical industry workforce needs. Additionally, we spotlight two organizations working to advance strong workplace climates that support attraction, retention, and long-term business performance within technical sectors:

- **Manufacturing:** Manufacturing Extension Partnerships, National Manufacturing Alliance
- **Construction:** Occupational Safety and Health Administration (OSHA), Construction Trades
- **Engineering:** American Society for Engineering Education (ASEE), National Association of Engineers

- **Toyota North America:** Toyota ranks fourth on Fair360's (formerly DiversityInc's Top 50) Companies for Diversity list.[13] Toyota has received 11 other recognitions, with some emphasizing Asian American, Black, Latinx, and LGBTQ+ employees. With the transition and legal aspects of DEI evolving, Toyota's 2024 annual report, entitled "D+I," primarily addresses the diversity and inclusion of the modern workforce.[14] Their priorities focus on creating a culture of belonging, learning, and development, as well as engaging with communities. Toyota maintains a self-reported dashboard of statistics to report workforce diversity, comprising 24 percent women, 34 percent minorities, 4 percent veterans, and 4 percent people with disabilities. Toyota's innovative programs include informal generational connections, mentoring, and synergistic partnerships (e.g., father–son processing companies).
- **Turner Construction:** Turner Construction[15] ranks #399 on the Forbes' diversity list of 2024.[16] Of the 500 companies highlighted, only three were construction-focused (as it relates to commercial buildings only). Turner emphasized diversity in their "Protect & Actively Care for People" section of their 2023 Strategic Plan.[17] The focus on equitable representation included diversifying access and awareness of construction by recruiting college students, participating in 12 student engagement events, incorporating a skill-based learning culture, and doing what they term "creating the right environment for employees." This plan segment takes a proactive approach to empower all individuals to reach their full potential, work daily to eliminate hate and bias from the industry, and enhance worker benefits.

There are long-standing perceptions within many technical industries that discourage new entrants and limit broader participation in the field. While some organizations are evolving their approaches to talent development and repositioning their workforce strategies, policy shifts and legal ambiguity are creating uncertainty for companies and employees. These dynamics will continue to shape how organizations communicate about workplace culture, values, and expectations moving forward.

Expanding talent access remains a competitive advantage in a global workforce landscape. Many organizations continue to adopt practices that support broader participation across multiple populations, not only related to race but also gender, skill background, career history, age, and pathways into technical work. One area requiring additional attention across technical sectors is the persistent pattern of "occupational sorting," where certain roles become clustered by gender over time. Addressing this pattern is essential to ensuring technical fields have access to the widest possible pool of talent capable of supporting innovation, productivity, and future workforce demands.

Meeting Future Workforce Needs

In light of recent shifts in national policy and workplace priorities, organizations still face urgent challenges related to the talent pipeline, workforce shortages, rapid technological disruption, and the evolving nature of work. While a single universal framework may not fully satisfy all perspectives, scholars and practitioners share responsibility for examining strategies that strengthen talent development and expand participation in technical industries. Employers (regardless of political climate) must still address how to attract, prepare, and retain a workforce capable of meeting present and future labor market demands.

This work will require reframing how talent is identified, recruited, and supported. Before hiring decisions are made, employers benefit from clarifying the specific skills required for success in open positions and determining where those skills might already exist in adjacent labor pools. Individuals transitioning from other technical fields, service sectors, retail, food industries, education, and public service roles often bring transferable strengths that can be leveraged and upskilled. Creating broader on-ramps into technical work expands the talent pool while also reducing time and cost associated with persistent vacancies.

As political landscapes evolve, definitions, expectations, and organizational policies may continue to shift. Despite this variability, there remains shared value in strengthening workforce capacity, building credible pathways into technical roles, and enabling individuals to thrive in workplaces where their strengths are recognized. Sustainable workforce strategies remain beneficial for employers, regional economies, and society as a whole.

Additional Reflections

- As policy environments and legal interpretations continue to shift, it remains important to stay engaged in constructive dialogue about how changes may influence talent development, workforce pipelines, and the capacity to bring more individuals into technical career fields.
- Historically, broadening access to education and employment opportunities has played a critical role in expanding who participates in the workforce. Continued attention to equitable access, both widening the number of people who enter the pipeline and broadening the range of backgrounds from which talent is sourced, can help address persistent labor shortages and strengthen productivity across technical industries.

Notes

1 American Bar Association (2021, January). What Is an Executive Order? https://www.americanbar.org/groups/public_education/publications/teaching-legal-docs/what-is-an-executive-order-/
2 Office of Federal Contract Compliance Programs (n.d.). *Executive Order 11246, As Amended.* OFCCP website.
3 Office of Federal Contract Compliance Programs (n.d.). *Section 503 of the Rehabilitation Act of 1973, As Amended.* OFCCP website.
4 Office of Federal Contract Compliance Programs (n.d.). *Vietnam Era Veterans' Readjustment Assistance Act of 1974, As Amended.* OFCCP website.
5 See Page, S. E. (2007). *The Difference: How the Power of Diversity Creates Better Groups, Firms, Schools, and Societies.* Princeton University Press; McMahon, A. M. (2010). Does Workplace Diversity Matter? A Survey of Empirical Studies on Diversity and Firm Performance, 2000–09. *Journal of Diversity Management (JDM)*, *5*(2). https://doi.org/10.19030/jdm.v5i2.808.
6 McKinsey & Company (2022). What Is Diversity, Equity, and Inclusion? https://www.mckinsey.com/featured-insights/mckinsey-explainers/what-is-diversity-equity-and-inclusion
7 Penn State University (n.d.). Retrieved from: https://studentaffairs.psu.edu/what-do-we-mean-diversity-equity-and-inclusion
8 University of Michigan (n.d.). *Defining Diversity, Equity and Inclusion.* https://odei.umich.edu/about/defining-dei/
9 U.S. Department of Education, Office of Inspector General (2022, September). *Diversity, Equity, Inclusion, and Accessibility Strategic Plan for Fiscal Years 2023–2028.* https://oig.ed.gov/sites/default/files/document/2023-02/ED%20OIG%20DEIA%20Strategic%20Plan%20FY%202023-2028.pdf
10 Office of Educational Equity (n.d.). Equity. Colorado Department of Higher Education. https://cdhe.colorado.gov/about-us/divisions/office-of-educational-equity
11 Deloitte University, Leadership Center for Inclusion (2023). *Unleashing the Power of Inclusion: Attracting and Engaging the Evolving Workforce.* https://www2.deloitte.com/content/dam/Deloitte/us/Documents/about-deloitte/us-about-deloitte-unleashing-power-of-inclusion.pdf
12 U.S. Government Accountability Office (January 2023). *Federal Workforce: Strengthening Diversity, Equity, Inclusion and Accessibility* [GAO-23–106254]. https://www.gao.gov/assets/gao-23-106254.pdf
13 Toyota North America (May 14, 2024). Toyota Ranks 4th on Fair360's Top 50 Companies. https://pressroom.toyota.com/toyota-ranks-4th-on-fair360s-top-50-companies/
14 Toyota (2024). Diversity + Inclusion 2024 Report. https://www.toyotaeffect.com/2024-d-i-annual-report/
15 Turner Construction (2024). Building Today to Transform Tomorrow. https://www.turnerconstruction.com/commitments/esg
16 Forbes (2024). Best Employers for Diversity. https://forbes.com/companies/turner-construction/?list=best-employers-diversity
17 Turner Construction (2023). *Turner 2023 Environmental, Social, and Governance Report.* https://issuu.com/turnerconstruction/docs/2023_esg_report?fr=sOWU4Yzc2MDI3MjQ

Chapter 4

Leadership Influence on Recruitment

Introduction to Leadership and Inclusivity

In modern organizational dynamics, leadership and inclusivity are intertwined concepts that play a pivotal role in shaping a progressive workplace. Leadership, in the context of inclusiveness, extends beyond mere management to inspire and cultivate a people-centered environment. It involves recognizing and valuing the unique backgrounds, perspectives, and abilities each individual brings to the table. Effective leaders are not only aware of the cultural, ethnic, and gender variances among their teams but also actively leverage these differences to foster innovation, creativity, and problem-solving. The importance of inclusion in the workplace cannot be overstated; it not only enhances decision-making quality by incorporating a wide range of viewpoints but also reflects the nature of global markets and communities. By embedding these principles into the core of organizational culture, leaders can create a vibrant, dynamic, and inclusive environment that not only respects but also celebrates the multifaceted fabric of its workforce.

Leaders take on the responsibility of being architects of change and must establish the organization's strategic design. Regardless of organizational size, the C-suite defines the comprehensive strategy, including mission, vision, and core values. To build and sustain a representative workforce, leaders must proactively ensure that equity-centered talent management is integrated and embedded across the organization's HR strategic, development, and operational foundations.

Leadership Identity

Leadership identity reflects how a leader understands who they are, how they show up, and how their lived experiences shape the way they lead others. Leaders bring their own backgrounds, values, strengths, assumptions, and expectations into the workplace. Because leadership heavily influences

DOI: 10.4324/9781003515937-5

culture and talent decisions, leaders benefit from deep self-reflection. These three questions help leaders articulate their identity more clearly and understand how their personal orientation affects recruitment, communication, decision-making, and workforce development.

In the strategic aspect, leaders are responsible for ensuring that inclusion remains at the forefront and that this commitment is intentionally woven throughout the organization. Based on our most recent research, we believe and have confirmed through preliminary qualitative case studies that leaders are the primary drivers of inclusivity within the organization. With that in mind, we begin with leadership on both the right and left sides of our Talent Expansion Framework. Specifically, we recommend gaining a better understanding of leaders and their influence on strategic recruitment. Referring back to the full Talent Expansion Framework (TXF) in Figure 4.1, the leadership actions flank both sides of the framework exterior to demonstrate the significance leaders have in grounding talent expansion by authorizing, designing, and implementing the recruitment plan, and ensuring its effectiveness and sustainability to support employee retention.

Setting the Tone for Inclusion

Setting the tone for inclusion within an organization begins at the top. Leaders have the unique responsibility not only to endorse but also to embody the values of inclusion in every aspect of organizational culture. It is their actions and attitudes that set the precedent for an environment where differences are not just accepted but valued and sought after. Leaders influence organizational culture by modeling respectful and collaborative behavior, setting clear expectations for fairness and inclusion, and ensuring these values are reflected in the organization's policies, practices, and goals. This leadership approach is crucial in establishing a workplace where all employees feel valued and empowered to contribute their best.

Most notably, research indicates that leaders need to understand their "leadership identity." From our research, we determined that specific areas were significant characteristics of leaders who successfully recruited and retained a diverse workforce. Figure 4.2 explores the leadership identity section of the TXF, where leaders can examine their connections to inclusivity and how it shapes their approach to talent expansion.

They can determine this by asking themselves a series of questions to inform their initial response to inclusive leadership. Reflecting on their perceptions of leadership may include a deeper exploration of their lived experiences. A more in-depth discussion of the leadership identity questions, along with specific reflections on individual leadership, is included.

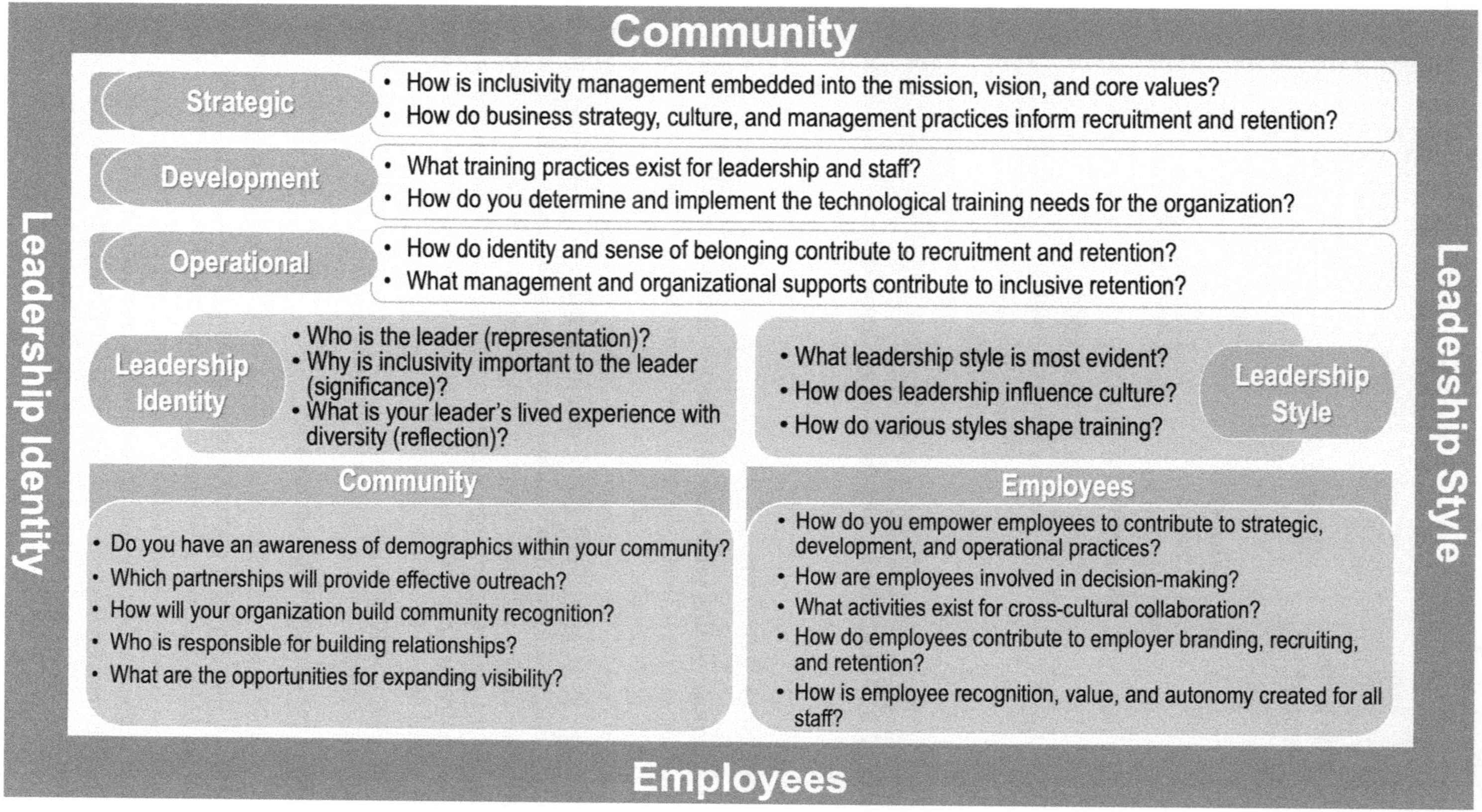

Figure 4.1 Talent Expansion Framework (TXF). Image Credit: Laurel A. Royer (2026)

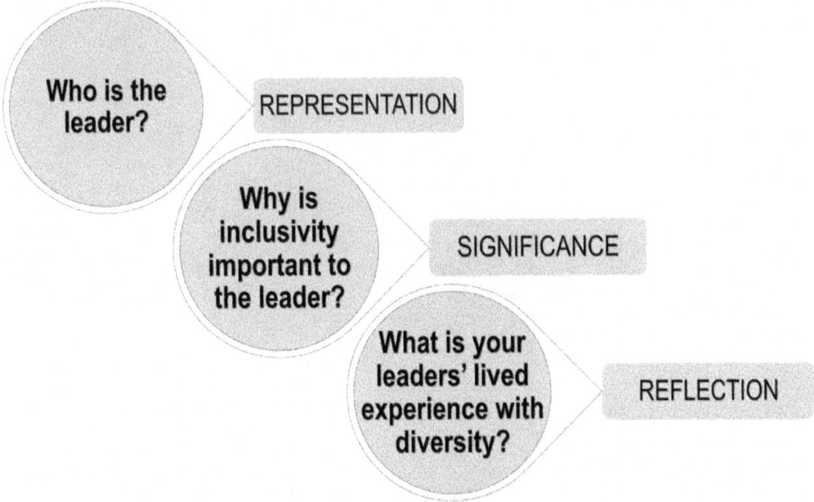

Figure 4.2 TXF Leadership Identity Focus. Image Credit: Laurel A. Royer (2026)

Leadership Questions

The purpose of this reflection is to better understand who the leader is, how they interpret their role, and how their personal values influence the way they lead people. These questions should be explored with leaders at every level of the organization, including executives, supervisors, and front-line managers. Leadership identity matters because leaders set the conditions, tones, and expectations that shape how teams work, how decisions are made, and how talent is supported. In a business environment marked by volatility, rapid change, and continuous adjustments, leaders who are intentional about their identity are more consistent, more adaptable, and more effective in shaping a strong workforce culture and talent development practices.

Who Is the Leader (Representation)?

Leadership representation reflects how a leader sees themselves in relation to those they serve. It includes their professional experience, role, position, and how they perceive their authority within the system. This requires leaders to consider what identities or perspectives they represent, and how those influence their credibility, communication, and approach to leading. When leaders understand their representation, they can more intentionally align their influence with the needs of the workforce.

QUESTION 1: WHO IS THE LEADER?

This question explores the characteristics of the leaders as they relate to their personal characteristics. From our research, how do they show up at work, and, specifically, what is their representation? We hear that representation matters, but does this only apply to race, gender, socioeconomic status, and overall background? Other factors are considerations, too. What area of the country or world are you from? Are there cultural, ethnic, or religious attributes that should be considered in influencing who they are as a leader? Most importantly, leaders are human too, and who they are influences how they connect, show bias, and overcome barriers to growth. Taking time to dive deeper into who the leader is matters. The racial demographic of leadership contributes to representation and advancement in leadership. If you are planning to attract and retain diverse talent, understanding who is in your leadership positions and who is in the pipeline will enable you to forecast your recruitment and promotion needs for diverse staffing.

Reflective Prompt:

How does your representation influence or contribute to the inclusivity of recruitment?

____

____

____

____

____

____

____

____

____

Why Is Inclusivity Important to the Leader (Significance)?

Each leader must examine the degree to which they believe broad participation, equitable access to opportunity, and fair treatment contribute to organizational success. Leaders who recognize the significance of inclusivity view talent development not as an optional add-on, but as a strategic business necessity tied to competitiveness, innovation, sustainability, and workforce stability. Understanding this significance clarifies why leaders choose to invest in practices that foster collaboration and shared growth.

QUESTION 2: WHY IS INCLUSIVITY IMPORTANT TO THE LEADER?

Our research indicates that leaders who have a connection to diversity or inclusion, either personally or professionally, are more open and committed to inclusive leadership. Therefore, we recommend gaining a deeper understanding of the leadership association and perspective.

Reflective Prompt:

How do your values influence or contribute to the inclusivity of recruitment?

____

____

____

____

____

____

____

____

____

What Is Your Leaders' Lived Experience in Diversity (Reflection)?

Leaders must reflect on their personal exposure, interactions, and experiences working alongside people whose backgrounds differ from their own. These lived experiences shape their awareness, openness to perspective-taking, and comfort level with navigating unfamiliar situations. The more leaders examine their real experiences, the more prepared they are to respond intentionally rather than reactively. Leaders grounded in this reality approach talent, conflict, and decision-making with greater humility and flexibility, supporting stronger workforce outcomes across the organization.

QUESTION 3: WHAT IS YOUR LEADERSHIP LIVED EXPERIENCE (REFLECTION)?

According to the authors' research and field interviews, leaders who have a positive association with and lived experience of diversity are more likely to adopt and be intentional about inclusive recruitment and retention, and to protect them as HR practices. As noted earlier, given leadership representation, lived experiences may differ across your leadership staff.

Reflective Prompt:
How has your lived experience positively or negatively influenced your association with inclusive recruitment? How often do you reflect on your lived experiences as a leader?

Authors' Tip #1: Revisit Lived Experiences to Gain Perspective on Your Association with Diversity

Leadership Values

As you continue to reflect on your leadership identity, we recommend you consider how your leadership values are enhancing or limiting your focus on recruitment efforts. Leadership values shape what a leader prioritizes, protects, communicates, and invests in. Values serve as the internal compass that influences the choices leaders make related to people, strategy, and organizational development. They reveal what leaders view as worth investing time, resources, and attention toward, especially when competing demands arise. Understanding leadership values helps determine whether leaders will support practices that broaden workforce participation and strengthen talent development. When leaders clearly articulate and align their values with the organization's long-term workforce goals, they are more likely to make consistent decisions that reinforce fairness, collaboration, respect, and opportunity. Leadership values are observable not through statements alone, but through the investments leaders choose to make, the expectations they set, and the priorities they elevate in action.

Reflective Prompt:
What values guide decisions related to people and workforce development?

The question helps clarify which beliefs drive the leader's choices. It reveals what they view as critical to developing people, building strong teams, and preparing the organization for future talent demands.

Reflective Prompt:

How do these values influence where time, resources, and attention are allocated?

Leaders demonstrate their values through the investments they make. Whether allocating funds, scheduling priorities, or determining strategic focus areas, resource decisions reflect what matters most to the leader.

Reflective Prompt:

How consistently are these values demonstrated through actions, investments, and priorities?

Values must be visible not only in messaging but also in practice. Consistency between stated values and observable leadership actions builds trust, credibility, and clarity for employees.

Authors' Tip #2: Adopt a Comfort Level with Continuous Self-Awareness

One of the most important commitments leaders can make to strengthen workforce culture and talent practices is to embrace ongoing reflection on how they lead. Leadership identity is not static; it evolves as leaders grow, encounter new challenges, and gain exposure to different people, perspectives, and contexts. Developing comfort with examining one's own assumptions, reactions, blind spots, and behavioral patterns allows leaders to adjust intentionally rather than operate on autopilot. This level of self-awareness is a core foundation for effective leadership because it supports consistent decision-making, builds trust, and enables leaders to respond to workforce needs with clarity and empathy.

Leadership Style

Leadership style represents the way leaders approach decision-making, communication, motivation, and workforce development. While an organization may have stated values and philosophies, the visible leadership behaviors demonstrated day-to-day are what people actually experience and respond to. Understanding leadership style helps organizations better interpret why certain practices succeed, why some environments operate more collaboratively than others, and how leaders influence the conditions in which people either thrive or struggle (see Figure 4.3).

What Leadership Style Is Most Evident?

Identifying the dominant style helps clarify the tone, expectations, and pace of work. Some leaders drive performance through inspiration, others through structure, and others through collaboration or autonomy. Naming the primary style makes it easier to evaluate whether the current approach supports the needs of the workforce and aligns with long-term organizational goals.

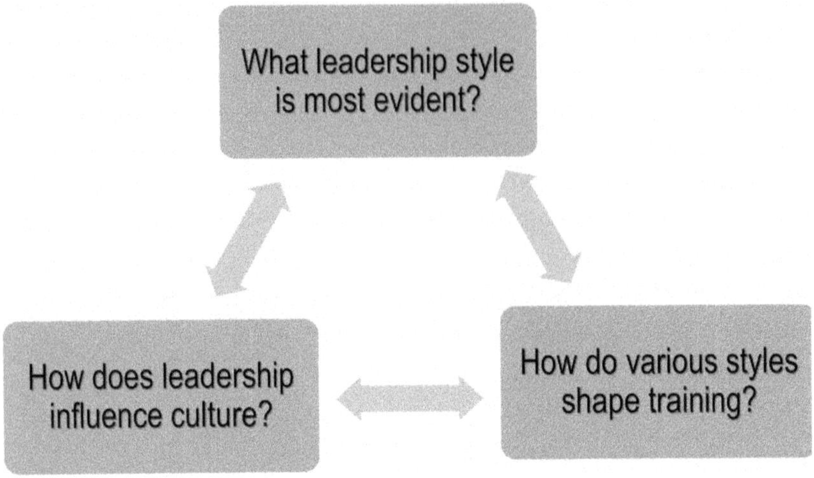

Figure 4.3 TXF Leadership Style Focus. Image Credit: Laurel A. Royer (2026)

How Does Leadership Influence Culture?

Leadership behaviors become cultural norms. The way leaders respond to challenges, uncertainty, feedback, and new ideas sends signals to the workforce about what is valued. Over time, these signals become the culture. Leaders who operate transparently, listen actively, and model fairness create a climate where employees are more willing to contribute, problem-solve, and stay engaged.

How Do Various Leadership Styles Shape Training?

Leadership style influences how learning occurs and how people develop skills. For example, a leader who emphasizes structure may prioritize standardized training and formal procedures, while a leader who values collaboration may encourage team-based problem-solving and peer learning. Understanding this connection allows organizations to intentionally design training that supports growth, strengthens talent pipelines, and prepares employees for advancing responsibilities.

Figure 4.4 summarizes several commonly discussed leadership styles and illustrates how each aligns with workforce culture, decision-making, and talent motivation. The purpose is not to assign a "right" or "wrong" style, but to recognize that leaders bring different orientations into their organizations, which shape how talent is attracted, supported, and developed within technical sectors.

Leadership Style	Core Focus	Decision-Making	Motivation Approach
Inclusive Leadership	Inspiring vision, innovation, and personal growth	Shared and participative; values all perspectives	Serves as the baseline; integrates elements of empathy, fairness, and collaboration from multiple styles
Transformational	Inspiring, rewards, and performance management	Empowering; encourages initiative under a shared vision	Adds explicit equity and belonging; ensures all voices are heard, not just inspired
Transactional	Structure, rewards, and performance management	Top-down; decisions tied to rules and results	Focuses on human connection over compliance and control
Servant Leadership	Serving others' needs and personal growth	Collaborative and people-first	Adds systemic fairness and inclusion structures beyond empathy
Autocratic	Control, authority, and efficiency	Centralized; leader makes all key decisions	Opposite; empowering, systemic, and psychologically safe
Relational	Participation, collaboration, and consensus	Motivates compliance and discipline	Opposite; empowering, participatory, and psychologically safe
Laissez-faire	Autonomy and minimal interference	Relies on intrinsic motivation and independence	Goes further by addressing systemic barriers to equal participation
Situational	Adapting style to context and maturity of followers	Relies on intrinsic motivation and independence	Consistently people-centered; ensures equity in all situations

Figure 4.4 Leadership Style Examples. Created by the Authors.

Readers can use the chart in Figure 4.4 as a self-reflection and calibration tool. Consider your natural tendencies, the tendencies of the leaders around you, and how these styles show up in daily decisions, hiring behaviors, and team development practices. Not every situation requires the same style, but understanding leadership preferences enables intentional adjustments tailored to context, workforce needs, and organizational goals. We encourage you to revisit this chart periodically, particularly when planning change efforts, building new teams, or reviewing talent development strategy, so that leadership behaviors intentionally strengthen fairness, collaboration, trust building, and long-term workforce growth.

Case Examples of Leadership Impact on Workforce Expansion

Case examples of effective talent expansion efforts consistently demonstrate the influence of senior leadership. In a global technology company, a new executive team prioritized strengthening talent pipelines and embedding continuous learning within the workforce culture. Leadership introduced scorecards connected to hiring outcomes and skill development benchmarks, ensuring managers were accountable for expanding access to technical roles. Over time, this approach supported increased mobility, encouraged the hiring of candidates with varying skill backgrounds, and fostered stronger cross-team collaboration. In another large enterprise technology firm, leadership commissioned a comprehensive internal compensation analysis after noticing patterns that signaled potential imbalance across employee groups. The organization invested in recalibrating salaries, embedded recurring audits into the business cycle, and transparently communicated the results to employees. This commitment reinforced trust and helped retain highly skilled workers, and established leadership accountability as a core business principle.

These examples illustrate how leadership commitment, paired with measurable accountability practices, can positively shape workforce development, strengthen recruitment outcomes, and enhance organizational performance.

Case Study Example: Advanced Manufacturing Firm: *A large, advanced manufacturing company underwent an organizational shift when new executive leadership prioritized building a culture of continuous learning to support operational excellence and workforce adaptability. Leaders implemented performance scorecards linked to recruitment outcomes, internal upskilling efforts, and cross-department collaboration. By doing so, managers were encouraged to expand talent sourcing approaches, support on-the-job skill development, and create clearer pathways for internal advancement. Over time, the organization experienced improvements in production efficiency, reduced turnover in skilled roles, and stronger innovation cycles across product lines.*

Case Study Example: Commercial Construction Contractor: *A national commercial construction firm conducted an internal assessment of compensation practices after concerns emerged regarding inconsistencies across job classifications and project divisions. Leadership initiated a compensation audit, adjusted salaries to align with role expectations, and formalized this review process as a recurring practice. This increased transparency improved employee confidence in leadership decisions, strengthened retention among experienced craft and technical workers, and signaled the company's commitment to fair workforce practices. These actions positioned the firm as a preferred employer and helped expand the pipeline of talent interested in advancing within the construction trades.*

Strategic Framework for Expanding Workforce Recruitment

Developing a strategic framework for strengthening recruitment begins with a clear understanding of the organization's existing workforce composition and current recruitment practices. This requires assessing relevant workforce data, examining representation across roles and levels of responsibility, and evaluating the effectiveness of existing sourcing channels. Establishing an accurate baseline allows organizations to identify strengths, gaps, and improvement opportunities that can better inform more intentional recruitment strategies.

The next step is to develop a vision for expanding and strengthening the talent pipeline that aligns with the organization's broader mission, industry competitiveness, and strategic growth priorities. This vision should clearly articulate the type of workforce the organization seeks to build and how this vision supports innovation, adaptability, and future workforce demands. The vision should be consistently communicated across the organization, so all stakeholders understand the purpose, expectations, and desired outcomes.

Finally, setting specific, measurable, and attainable goals is essential for translating strategy into practice. These goals should include benchmarks that reflect business priorities and guide recruitment decision-making. Goals may also include timelines and indicators for evaluating progress. It is equally important that the goals consider the full employee lifecycle, including hiring, retention, development, and advancement. Establishing clear objectives enables organizations to monitor outcomes, adjust practices as needed, and maintain accountability for strengthening workforce recruitment in a fair, consistent, and sustainable manner.

Leadership plays a critical role in driving recruitment strategy. Leaders at every level (executive, mid-level, operational, and supervisory) shape culture, influence implementation, and hold responsibility for aligning recruitment practices with long-term talent needs. Understanding leadership perspectives, values, and decision-making approaches can help organizations gain insight into how to support stronger recruitment and workforce development practices across the enterprise.

Leadership Approaches to Strengthen Fair and Balanced Recruitment

Effective leadership in recruitment requires a multifaceted strategy, beginning with leading by example. Leaders should model fairness, consistency, and open-mindedness in their hiring practices to set the tone for the organization. This includes seeking out a wide range of qualified candidates and ensuring that hiring decisions are made objectively and free from bias. Leaders demonstrate commitment not only through policy but also through actions such as participating in outreach events or professional groups that broaden access to talent. By doing so, they reinforce that fairness and equity are organizational priorities that shape culture and encourage others to do the same.

Developing and implementing transparent and unbiased recruitment policies and practices are essential to attracting and retaining top talent. Leaders should ensure recruitment processes are structured to minimize barriers and provide equal consideration to all candidates. This may involve revising job descriptions to focus on essential skills, using structured interview questions, and employing consistent evaluation criteria. Regularly reviewing and updating these processes ensures alignment with evolving expectations around fairness and organizational integrity. A continued commitment to refining recruitment practices signals a leader's dedication to building a workforce based on merit and mutual respect.

Investing in training and development that strengthen equitable recruitment practices is another key leadership approach. Leaders and HR teams should participate in professional learning focused on recognizing bias, improving cultural awareness, and communicating with fairness and clarity.

Such training equips decision-makers with the insight and tools to ensure hiring processes remain objective and inclusive of a broad range of perspectives. Moreover, cultivating future leaders who are skilled in equitable hiring practices supports the organization's long-term success. Ongoing training and reflection help leaders adapt to changing workforce needs and sustain a culture that values fairness, transparency, and respect at every level.

Instruments for Informed Decision-Making

Effective leadership in recruitment requires not only a commitment to inclusion but also self-awareness and an understanding of team dynamics. Leaders who use personality assessments can make more informed decisions by understanding their own behavioral preferences and those of others, which can help create an inclusive environment where talent thrives. Two popular tools, the Myers-Briggs Type Indicator (MBTI)[1] and the DiSC®,[2] offer valuable insights into leadership styles and team dynamics, enhancing recruitment efforts.

Myers-Briggs

Understanding personality differences through tools such as the MBTI can be pivotal in how leaders approach recruitment. The MBTI helps leaders identify their own personality preferences across four dimensions (Extraversion/Introversion, Sensing/Intuition, Thinking/Feeling, and Judging/Perceiving) and recognize how these preferences influence their leadership style. For instance, an introverted leader may prefer one-on-one interactions and need to be more mindful of engaging with candidates in a more open manner. In contrast, a feeling-oriented leader might naturally focus on interpersonal connections and the well-being of candidates. By understanding both their own MBTI type and the types of others, leaders can better appreciate various perspectives, enhance team dynamics, and make more balanced recruitment decisions that are sensitive to different communication styles and work preferences. This self-awareness fosters inclusive recruitment practices, ensuring that no candidate is inadvertently excluded due to personality-based biases.

DiSC

Another useful tool for informed decision-making in leadership is the DiSC personality assessment. DiSC focuses on four primary behavioral traits: Dominance (D), Influence (I), Steadiness (S), and Conscientiousness (C). This model helps leaders understand their behavioral tendencies and how they respond to challenges, influence others, maintain pace, and adhere to rules. For example, a leader with a high Dominance trait may be decisive and task-oriented, which is beneficial in fast-paced recruitment environments. However, they may need to ensure their drive for quick decisions does not overlook the nuances of recruitment, such as adequately considering underrepresented candidates. Conversely, leaders with high Influence may excel at engaging and inspiring candidates, but they must also balance their enthusiasm with careful evaluation of each candidate's qualifications. Understanding the various DiSC profiles enables leaders to communicate more effectively, reduce bias in decision-making, and develop inclusive recruitment strategies that reflect the varied needs and preferences of candidates. By integrating DiSC insights, leaders can adapt their approach to create a welcoming environment where various personalities feel valued and understood. Both MBTI and DiSC offer leaders tools to better understand themselves and their teams, providing critical insights into how personality influences workplace behavior. When applied thoughtfully, these instruments help leaders enhance recruitment by fostering self-awareness, improving communication, and cultivating a more inclusive and dynamic organizational culture.

Active Participation of Leaders in Recruitment

Active leadership participation in equitable recruitment practices is essential to the success of equity-centered initiatives. Engaging directly with underrepresented communities and talent pools is one effective way leaders can demonstrate this commitment. This may include participating in career fairs at minority-serving institutions, partnering with organizations or educational institutions that support historically underrepresented groups, and utilizing expanded sourcing channels to reach a wider range of applicants. Leaders can also leverage their personal and professional networks to broaden candidate access. By intentionally seeking out and engaging with talent across varied backgrounds and experiences, leaders not only expand the organization's reach but also signal a genuine commitment to building and sustaining an inclusive and representative workforce.

Collaborating with human resources (HR) is key to effectively implementing equitable recruitment strategies. Leaders and HR professionals must work together to align equity-focused recruitment goals with the organization's overall business strategy and HR practices. This collaboration may include developing clear policies and procedures that support equitable hiring, designing training programs for hiring managers, and establishing metrics to evaluate the effectiveness of recruitment and retention efforts. By combining their expertise and resources, leaders and HR can create a more cohesive and comprehensive approach to building a representative workforce. This partnership ensures that the organization's commitment to equity is not simply stated in its mission but is also reflected in its day-to-day operations and practices.

Overcoming challenges and barriers in recruitment requires both resilience and innovation from leaders. Equity-focused workforce initiatives often encounter obstacles such as unconscious bias, resistance to change, and limited candidate pipelines within specific sectors. Leaders must therefore take a proactive role in identifying underlying barriers and implementing strategic solutions to address them. This may involve investing in bias training, seeking external advice or partnerships to broaden talent pools, and consistently evaluating and adapting recruitment practices. Leaders must also be prepared to address any resistance within the organization, championing the importance of inclusion and demonstrating its value to the organization's success. By being adaptable and committed, leaders can navigate these challenges and play a pivotal role in creating a more inclusive workplace.

Advocacy Beyond Recruitment

Advocacy extends well beyond the initial recruitment phase, requiring leaders to focus on long-term strategies for maintaining and nurturing a representative workforce. This involves not only bringing in new talent, but also supporting employee retention, growth, and career development. Leaders play a crucial role in cultivating an inclusive environment where all employees feel valued and have equitable opportunities for advancement. Implementing mentorship programs, offering career development workshops, and ensuring transparent and fair promotion processes are examples of practices that help foster this inclusivity. In addition, the effectiveness of recruitment and retention efforts should be continuously evaluated through meaningful indicators such as employee turnover rates, satisfaction scores, and representation across levels of the organization. These measures provide tangible evidence of impact, allowing leaders to refine strategies and demonstrate a sustained commitment to building and maintaining an inclusive workplace.

Leaders Championing Fair and Balanced Recruitment

Many organizations have set powerful examples of fairness and inclusion through leadership-driven initiatives. A case study from Harvard Business School highlights a key lesson on breaking cycles of uniformity in leadership roles.[3] The research emphasizes that when individuals from a variety of backgrounds and experiences take on positions traditionally held by a narrow group, it strengthens organizational innovation and adaptability. This finding underscores the importance of leaders who actively broaden participation and encourage a mix of perspectives within their teams.

Additionally, Diversio demonstrates the benefits of leadership that champions fairness and inclusion, particularly when supported by data-informed strategies and measurable goals.[4] Organizations that implement these approaches not only cultivate stronger team engagement but also achieve measurable improvements in performance and decision-making. Evidence-based recruitment and leadership practices help ensure that fairness, opportunity, and innovation become embedded within the organization's culture and operations.

These examples collectively show that effective leadership for equitable recruitment requires both challenging outdated patterns and adopting transparent, data-driven methods that produce tangible outcomes. Leaders who commit to these principles play a critical role in ensuring that fairness and inclusion are not just aspirations, but enduring qualities of their organizational culture and practice.

Reflective Prompt:

What can you do as a fair and collaborative leader to strengthen equitable recruitment within your organization?

___

___

___

___

___

___

___

___

___

HR Action Step: Assess Your Leadership Bias

Taking a self-assessment of bias can be beneficial, such as the Harvard Implicit Bias Test.[5] This online tool helps in identifying unconscious preferences and biases related to race, gender, sexual orientation, and other aspects. By understanding these biases, leaders can better understand how they might influence their recruitment and leadership practices, and commit to ongoing personal development in this area.

HR Action Step: Continue Leadership Development (Informally)

To further strengthen leadership effectiveness, leaders can engage in ongoing professional learning activities such as attending leadership and organizational culture workshops, reading books and articles on collaboration and cultural awareness, or participating in training programs that enhance understanding of workplace dynamics. For example, joining webinars hosted by respected industry experts or following thought leaders on equitable hiring and leadership practices can provide valuable insights and broaden perspectives.

Building on this foundation, leaders can work with HR to create outreach strategies that expand access to a wide range of qualified candidates. This may include partnering with professional associations and educational institutions that serve underrepresented or specialized talent pipelines—such as Asian American and Native American Pacific Islander-Serving Institutions (ANNAPISIs), Alaska Native and Native Hawaiian-Serving Institutions (ANNHs), Historically Black Colleges and Universities (HBCUs), Hispanic-Serving Institutions (HSIs), Native American-Serving Nontribal Institutions (NASNTIs), Predominantly Black Institutions (PBIs), and Tribal Colleges and Universities (TCUs). These partnerships can help organizations connect with a broader spectrum of emerging professionals while reinforcing their commitment to equitable opportunity and leadership excellence.

HR Action Step: Develop Data Analysis Skills

The strategy could also include analyzing recruitment data to identify trends and gaps in the hiring process. During this step, it is important to understand current baseline data and consider how key metrics can be expanded to strengthen equitable hiring practices. It is also essential to engage with multiple communities and professional networks to increase the visibility of job openings, which helps broaden the applicant pool. This may involve participating in career fairs at minority-serving institutions, partnering with organizations that support historically underrepresented groups within the industry, or hosting targeted recruitment events aligned to specific workforce needs.

Tools

Once you have identified a strong and varied pool of applicants, it is a good time to implement fair and bias-reducing practices in hiring. This may include adopting structured interview processes where all candidates are asked the same set of questions to ensure a consistent and equitable evaluation process. Using hiring panels that include individuals with a range of perspectives can also help reduce personal bias. Ongoing evaluation of recruitment efforts is essential for continuous improvement. This can include regularly reviewing recruitment metrics to assess candidate outreach, interview experiences, and hiring outcomes, and then adjusting strategies as needed to meet organizational goals.

After new hires have joined the organization, it is equally important to focus on retention through effective mentoring and sponsorship. Leaders can establish mentorship programs where experienced employees guide newer team members, helping them navigate the workplace culture and advance in their careers. Sharing best practices and lessons learned through internal platforms or professional forums can help strengthen equitable recruitment and retention strategies.

Beyond the hiring process, leaders should work to cultivate a respectful and collaborative organizational culture by modeling fairness, transparency, and accountability. Encouraging an environment where all employees feel valued and able to contribute their best work helps sustain long-term engagement and success. Finally, leaders should advocate for policies and practices that support not only recruitment but also the retention and advancement of talent across all levels of the organization.

Conclusion

In conclusion, the evolving role of leadership in fostering fairness, collaboration, and broad organizational engagement is a critical component of modern success. Key takeaways from this discussion emphasize that effective leaders must not only support equitable practices but also actively model and reinforce them, ensuring these values are embedded within the organization's culture. From setting the tone for a respectful and inclusive environment to implementing transparent recruitment and development strategies, leaders play a central role in cultivating workplaces where all individuals can thrive. Looking ahead, leaders and organizations must continue to adapt and refine their approaches to align with changing workforce dynamics and societal expectations. This ongoing commitment calls for proactive leadership at every level, championing fairness, accountability, and belonging as essential drivers of organizational resilience, innovation, and long-term growth.

Putting It into Practice

Reflect on Your Leadership Approach: Regularly assess how your values, communication, and decision-making shape your leadership. Seek feedback from trusted colleagues and remain open to growth and perspective-taking.

Strengthen Fair and Consistent Hiring Practices: Use structured interviews, clear rubrics, and transparent evaluation criteria to ensure consistency and fairness in hiring and advancement decisions.

Build Broad Professional Connections: Engage with a variety of professional networks and communities to widen your perspective and discover new sources of insight and talent.

Invest in Mentorship and Professional Growth: Support the next generation of leaders by mentoring colleagues, offering guidance, and opening doors for growth opportunities.

Review and Refine Team Development Efforts: Regularly evaluate how well your team's recruitment, onboarding, and retention strategies are working, and make evidence-based improvements.

Foster a Culture of Belonging and Respect: Model empathy, collaboration, and psychological safety. Encourage open dialogue and ensure every voice has the opportunity to contribute.

Exchange Ideas and Successful Practices: Collaborate across departments and organizations to share lessons learned and approaches that strengthen team performance and engagement.

Lead by Example at Every Level: Demonstrate inclusive leadership through your actions by advocating for fairness, transparency, and growth for all members of your organization.

Notes

1 Myers-Briggs Company (n.d.). Retrieved from https://www.themyersbriggs.com/
2 Everything DiSC (n.d.). Retrieved from https://www.everythingdisc.com/
3 Blanding, M. (2024). Want to Make Diversity Stick? Break the Cycle of Sameness. Working Knowledge, Harvard Business School. https://www.library.hbs.edu/working-knowledge/want-to-make-diversity-stick-break-the-sameness-cycle
4 Fellows, D. (2024, November 26). Inclusive Leadership in British Companies: Data-Driven Insights for the C-suite. Diversio. https://diversio.com/inclusive-leadership-british-companies/
5 You can access the test at https://implicit.harvard.edu/implicit/

Chapter 5

Strategic HR Practices for Recruitment

This chapter provides an overview of how strategic human resource (HR) practices shape organizational recruitment, retention, and long-term talent expansion. We begin by clarifying the distinctions between strategic, development, and operational HR functions and why these levels must work together to support inclusive and sustainable hiring. The chapter then explains the significance of strategic HR in a changing labor landscape, particularly as organizations adapt to automation, shifting market demands, and talent shortages. Through case examples and analysis, we introduce the Talent Expansion Framework (TXF) and new concepts such as *HR in Pieces*, the *HR Collective*, and the *HR Co-active* to illustrate how misalignment or synergy in HR practices can influence recruitment outcomes. Finally, the chapter concludes with actionable steps leaders can implement to strengthen recruitment strategies, hiring protocols, and organizational readiness for inclusive talent management. By previewing the strategic foundation and practical tools that follow, this chapter prepares readers to understand how HR strategy directly informs effective and inclusive workforce development.

Strategic, development, and operational HR practices occur at various levels of the organizational hierarchy, both singularly and in overlapping combinations. Strategic practices are embedded at the leadership level, where mission, vision, and core values guide people, production, and performance. HR development or training practices typically occur at the CEO/ownership and supervisory levels, where training coordinators may or may not be present. At the operational level, all leaders are required to be engaged where retention is a pain point. These three areas of HR practice should be designed, developed, and implemented in a way that enables leaders to monitor them, ensuring consistent, inclusive recruitment and voluntary retention. However, despite their best intentions, many companies struggle to embed effective inclusive management practices into their talent management. Research consistently shows that more diverse and inclusive workforces are associated with improved organizational performance[1] and

DOI: 10.4324/9781003515937-6

higher employee retention.[2] Therefore, companies need to develop HR strategic management practices that can contribute to holistic, sustainable talent management. To guide HR leaders and C-suite leaders on how HR strategic practices can inform recruitment, it is necessary to examine how HR is practiced.

Significance of Strategic HR Practices (Why)

The emergence of automation requires a shift in how we work. Strategic HR practices provide the context, purpose, and foundation for how humans, robots, and other technologies will interact and achieve success in prospective industries. At this level, a realignment of HR practices is necessary to ensure that impactful changes occur throughout the transformation, during which leaders may revisit their mission, vision, and core values, adapting them to meet the diverse needs of their workforce. Specific attention should be given to details related to the incorporation of new technologies, leadership transparency, and hiring practices. This section examines how strategic HR practices shape recruitment and retention and identifies who is responsible for implementing them to ensure they remain central to the company's commitment.

With the changing landscape of automation, firms should adopt a "ready, set, go" approach to attract, recruit, and retain diverse talent. By "ready, set, go," we mean a proactive sequence in which firms assess their current capacity, prepare intentional recruitment strategies, and then execute timely actions to strengthen and diversify their talent pipeline. Organizational agility ensures a company continues to progress, despite influences of policy, practice, and performance. When effective leaders implement intentional and effective HR strategic practices, they provide a blueprint for achieving inclusive excellence. When leaders individually and jointly strengthen their strategic HR skills, they will be better equipped to address the challenges posed by technological shifts, talent shortages, and new market entrants. Strategic practices elevate an organization from just a "simple" employer to a talent builder. Within technical industries, talent is scarce; however, a strategy that extends from entry-level roles at the ground floor to high-level leadership demonstrates an equitable approach to retention and succession planning. The intentionality of strategic practices prepares the leadership, organizational culture, and staff to engage in inclusive talent management. Our goal is to demonstrate that inclusive talent expansion is accessible to all organizations, regardless of size, and that the responsibility lies across the entire organization. While we agree that leaders drive change, when implemented effectively, every member of the organization has both the authority and the responsibility to ensure that effective change occurs.

With the proper strategy, training, and operational practices, attracting, recruiting, and retaining diverse talent is attainable.

Significance of Strategic HR Practices (Who)

Although the primary role of human resources management (HRM) typically falls to the owner, president, and C-suite professionals, we argue that there is a mutual shared responsibility for leaders at the mid and supervisory level to be connected to the HR strategic practices. Specifically, the decisions for how HR functions are determined from the mission, vision, core values, and general buy-in, but also the supervisors are the leaders who need to understand, implement, and retain accountability for the HRM outcomes. Similarly, the employees are charged with navigating complex HR processes to ensure proper policies, compliances, and safety standards are met. Since the strategic HR practices drive the cyclical nature of both HR development and operational practices, all leaders should be well-versed and fully prepared to identify, translate, probe, and challenge strategic HR practices. In the context of the TXF, the strength of the framework is the authority, accountability, and actions bestowed to all interest holders involved in the recruitment and retention process. Therefore, all companies should reconsider their position of HR as being "to protect the company" or "to protect the employees." We argue that no boundary should be drawn on who should engage with HR and its benefits. HR strategic practices should be adhered to and influenced by both leaders and staff as a catalyst for individual and collective growth. One leader intentionally allows all members of the organization to contribute to the mission, vision, and core values annually, and as preferred. By inviting a dialogue and being willing to engage in discourse about current and future HR strategies, each individual builds the organization they want to be part of. By securing more than just leadership buy-in, staff feel comfortable interacting during times of challenge and opportunity.

Reflective Prompt:

How often do you engage in discussion of strategic HR practices organization-wide?

____

____

____

____

____

____

Reflective Prompt:

What type of consistent coaching do you offer leaders (upper, mid-, and supervisory) to ensure they are confident in HR strategic practices?

Reflective Prompt:

What policies, programs, and evaluation processes inform cultural practices and culturally responsive decision-making efforts?

Significance of Strategic HR Practices (What)

Strategic human resource management refers to the intentional alignment of HR policies, practices, and systems with an organization's broader mission, vision, and long-term goals. Rather than functioning as a purely administrative unit, strategic HR serves as a driver of organizational performance, workforce sustainability, and competitive advantage. This includes integrating areas such as talent acquisition, professional development, performance management, and employee engagement into a cohesive system that supports both operational needs and future growth. Foundational resources that inform this approach include texts such as Armstrong's *Handbook of Human Resource Management Practice* and *Strategic Human Resource Management* by Jeffrey A. Mello, along with practitioner-oriented frameworks from the Society for Human Resource Management. These resources emphasize evidence-based decision-making, alignment with organizational strategy, and the importance of measuring HR outcomes to ensure impact.

Building on this foundation, the "what" of strategic HR practices centers on how these aligned systems show up in daily operations and decision-making. Inclusive talent management matters because it expands access to diverse skill sets, strengthens innovation, and improves retention by ensuring employees see pathways for growth and belonging. Business strategy directly informs inclusive management by shaping workforce planning, identifying critical roles, and determining how talent pipelines are developed and sustained. Organizational culture reflects the lived experience of these strategies, requiring ongoing assessment to determine whether values such as equity, transparency, and accountability are truly embedded in practice. Finally, HR management systems including policies for attraction, recruitment, and retention must be intentionally designed, regularly evaluated, and continuously improved to ensure they are equitable, compliant, and responsive to both employee and organizational needs.

Key Resources for Strategic HR Practices

- **Society for Human Resource Management (SHRM):** Toolkits, competency models, and guidance on strategic HR, talent management, and workplace culture. http://shrm.org/home
- **Gallup:** Evidence-based research on employee engagement, retention, and organizational culture. https://www.gallup.com/workplace/349484/state-of-the-global-workplace.aspx
- **CIPD:** Global perspective on people management, HR strategy, and professional development. https://www.cipd.co.uk/
- **WorldatWork:** Resources on compensation, total rewards, and performance alignment. https://worldatwork.org/
- ***Harvard Business Review*:** Practitioner-focused articles on leadership, culture, and strategic HR practices. https://hbr.org/

Strategic HR Management

Strategic human resource management (HRM) involves identifying an organization's HR functions and ensuring that HR plans align with the business strategy to achieve its long-term goals. Strategic oversight may vary by size, as smaller firms may not have the capacity to hire a larger leadership team and may rely on a single HR manager or office manager for assistance. When a smaller firm is involved and may not even have an HR "Department of One," the owner should consider accessing an expert for just-in-time, recruiting services, such as through the Chamber of Commerce or other professional associations. The strategic guidance is a pivotal aspect of recruitment that should be presented early in the company's development. At larger firms, strategic management efforts often occur across a core team of leaders responsible for various functions. The amplification of opinions can negatively impact process implementation or decision-making. While decisions are made at the C-suite level, theoretical and practical applications suggest that line-level managers, including supervisors, superintendents, field staff, and project managers, should be involved in the planning, execution, and operation of programs, policies, and procedures.

Overall, inclusive talent management is not a natural management skill. For some management professionals, it has been a steep learning curve. However, research indicates that effective HR practices can facilitate the communication necessary for activating an organization's commitment to inclusion. Before exploring other elements of the HR strategy for talent expansion, we outline the approach we took to investigate strategic management through a case study approach.

Strategic Management (Organization-Wide)

After interviewing several leaders in technical industries that exemplify inclusivity within their organizations, we found that their individual perspectives were strong drivers of how they ran their companies and utilized inclusivity as a strategic pillar. Below are four areas that have been prominent cornerstones of business success, along with tips for implementing these practices. These four areas of strategic HR practices form the basis for the TXF (see Figure 5.1). This framework guides the intentional, inclusive expansion of talent.

To address the strategic components of the TXF, leaders need to individually and collectively reflect on the broad-level questions addressed below.

- **Inclusive Talent Management:** Why does it matter?
- **Business Strategy:** How does the business strategy inform inclusive management?
- **Organizational Culture:** What is the current state of your organizational culture?
- **HR Management:** What policies exist for attraction, recruitment, and retention?

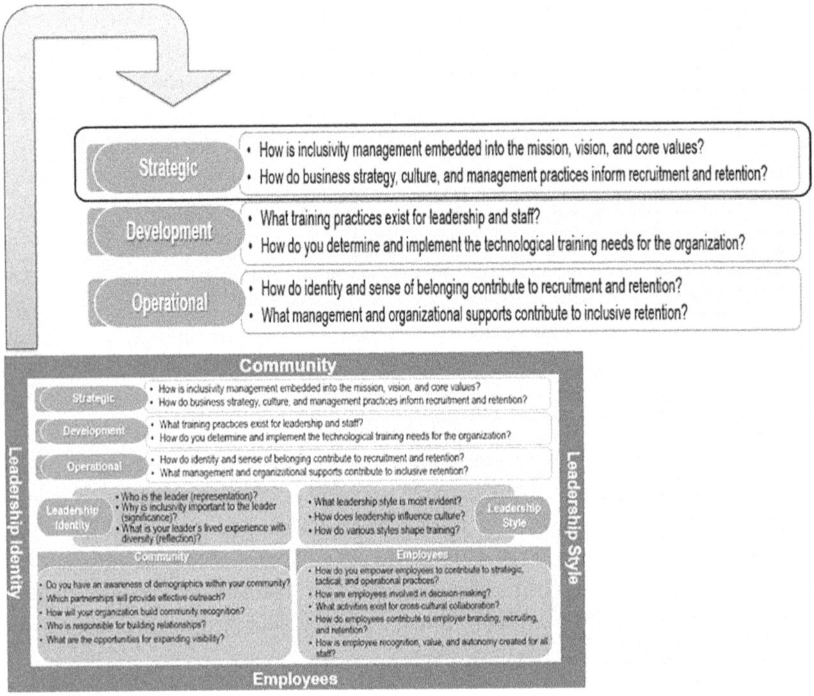

Figure 5.1 Strategic Focus of Talent Expansion Framework. Image Credit: Laurel A. Royer (2026)

These reflection questions serve as a diagnostic tool for organizations committed to strategic talent expansion. By examining why inclusive talent management matters to your specific context, you create a compelling business case that resonates with stakeholders at all levels. Understanding how your business strategy directly informs your approach to inclusion ensures alignment between organizational goals and talent initiatives, preventing them from becoming isolated or performative efforts. A candid assessment of your current organizational culture reveals both strengths to leverage and barriers to dismantle, providing an honest baseline from which to measure progress. Finally, evaluating existing HR management practices, particularly around attraction, recruitment, and retention, illuminates the systems, processes, and structures that either support or hinder inclusive talent development. Together, these questions move leaders beyond surface-level commitments toward a deep, strategic examination of how inclusion can become genuinely embedded in organizational DNA, driving both innovation and sustainable competitive advantage.

Why Does Inclusive Management Matter?

In a globally competitive job market, it is not enough to have a team with only the skills to perform the role. They must be able to perform the role effectively and engage collaboratively with both internal staff and external customers. In our research, inclusion matters as part of the overall business case (what's best for the organization), and leadership values (influenced by individual leadership identity and style) act as a lever to unlock latent shortages through inclusive hiring practices. It is important to note that we are focused on all dimensions of inclusion, not solely the race-based conversations that often dominate public discourse. Our framework encompasses inclusion across ability, thought, experience, background, and perspective, recognizing that true organizational strength emerges from the full spectrum of human differences.

Amidst criticism of inclusion initiatives, there remains considerable confusion surrounding affirmative action and talent expansion. Therefore, we will set these terminologies aside and address what will lead to holistic talent expansion, including how to improve talent depth (all talent that enters the workforce) and talent breadth (continuously strengthening the skills of the talent that exists in the field). In this book, we will address the adoption of inclusivity in technical industries and how we believe it can be implemented and led within sectors that represent the cornerstone of the US economy in the 21st century. In this chapter, we will adhere to our usual "who, what, and why" scenario. When we refer to the "who" in talent expansion management, we need to consider the "who of management," those who lead, plan, and influence effectively within the organization.

The business case for inclusive talent expansion includes customer expectations and satisfaction, workforce productivity, and innovation. Research indicates the business case for expanding talent pools, but why? A case study of a small business manufacturing company found that incorporating ideas from various backgrounds is beneficial for customers. However, historical recommendations and decisions in this area have demonstrated success from both theoretical (research-based) and practical (customer-oriented) contexts.

Case Study Example: *We believe in the old adage that "the customer is always right," and in technical industries like manufacturing, engineering, and construction, the quality of the work speaks for itself. With good craftsmanship, the technician, field worker, and imagineer always feel a sense of belonging in the industry. They take pride in their work, production, and contributions to their community. Customers purchase products when they feel comfortable with the message and the vision of an organization. We can relate to the "human side" of the product. We strive to work with companies that share our values: commonality, sustainability, responsibility, and accountability. When our workers come from diverse backgrounds, including various races, genders, ethnicities, and marginalized communities, customers are more willing to support the product.*

How Does Inclusive Business Strategy Inform Management?

How does your external business strategy represent management? Are you recognized as an organization that attracts, recruits, and supports diverse populations, including those of racial, cultural, gender, and special backgrounds? How do your mission, vision, and core values demonstrate your commitment to inclusivity internally? While recent shifts in the broader political environment have led many organizations to approach inclusion commitments with greater caution, the long-term benefits of embedding inclusive practices into a company's culture remain clear and continue to strengthen talent expansion and workforce readiness for the future of work. In the next section we will attempt to explain the historical aspects of successful talent integration for any organization seeking to understand its benefits and the integration process.

Community Visibility

All companies that have positive, impactful, inclusive talent management strategies for expansion do so intentionally. Their outreach and recruitment efforts are visible in local, regional, and statewide communities, the public at large, and their organizations. While you may have typically heard this referred to as a company brand, the word "brand" does not fully capture the extent to which these leaders aim to amplify inclusive talent expansion, not just as a key consideration but as the *only* consideration. We have renamed this approach to intentional company branding and recruitment as "Magnifying Company Ethos." When a company takes this approach, it embodies its ethos based on a set of diverse and inclusive principles. Through the intentional adoption of internal practices guided by core beliefs, character-building guidelines, and moral values that are equitable for all.

HR Action Step: "Magnify Company Ethos"

To magnify company ethos, organizations should embed inclusive talent practices into their core values, particularly the mission and vision that guide how customers, staff, and communities understand the company's identity. This approach moves beyond the mechanics of communication (e.g., email, phone) and emphasizes the broader message leaders send about what the organization stands for and how it shows up in the community.

Case Study Example: *A CEO of a manufacturing company actively participates in chamber of commerce meetings and serves on nonprofit boards to strengthen community impact, expand visibility, and better understand how the firm can influence and improve job quality.*

This case example is intended to show how visible, values-driven leadership reinforces an organization's ethos and strengthens trust within the community. Readers should take away that this intentional engagement, whether through local partnerships, civic involvement, or industry networks, signals a company's commitment to inclusive talent practices. Applying this insight means ensuring that leaders at all levels are present, accessible, and aligned with the organization's core values so that recruitment and workforce relationships extend beyond transactions and become part of the company's broader identity.

What Is the Current State of Organizational Culture?

While technological evolutions are trending towards outcome-based business practices, the human-centric aspects of our work will continue to support our operational approach. Research, practice, and experience demonstrate that leaders are drivers of organizational culture. However, taking the pulse of organizational culture regarding inclusive talent management is a necessary practice that requires both strategic and change management skills.

Evaluating Talent Management and Organizational Equity

As organizations refine their strategies for attracting and retaining a broad range of talent, leaders should recognize that there is no one-size-fits-all approach. By this, we mean that talent practices must be adapted to each organization's unique culture, workforce needs, and operational realities rather than assuming a single model will work effectively in every setting. In today's environment, political considerations, leadership perspectives, and existing organizational structures all influence decisions related to workforce management. Debate continues around how best to evaluate the effectiveness of fairness and inclusion training, particularly in measuring its long-term impact. Leaders who are committed to equitable and transparent talent practices remain open to learning new approaches and refining their methods over time. Executives and managers should prioritize active listening and regular communication to understand employees' and leaders' readiness to evolve policies and practices that shape recruitment and advancement.

HR Action Step: Assess the Organization's Readiness for Change

Before implementing any change researchers and practitioners recommend assessing an organization's readiness to change. Several industry experts in automation in manufacturing and construction have developed digital readiness assessments to address the transition to technologies. Refer to Chapter 1 for a starting point for assessing current hiring practices. All leaders, from the CEO to front-line leaders, must agree on how inclusion will be integrated into organizational practices. Since this is not a business management book per se, we will not provide a detailed examination of change management practices. However, in keeping with the theme of tips and resources, we would like to share models that can be useful for implementing the practices. These four areas of strategic HR practices form the foundation for this work.

As previously noted, to accommodate all the elements of strategic HR practices each interest holder (leaders, staff, community, and even competitors) may contribute to the designing, developing, and reorganizing of the mission, vision, and core values of the organization. Building on this foundation, the chapter emphasizes that strategic, development, and operational HR practices must work in alignment to create a cohesive system that supports inclusive recruitment, retention, and long-term talent expansion. Through the Talent Expansion Framework (TXF), organizations are encouraged to move beyond isolated HR actions and instead adopt integrated, organization-wide approaches that connect business strategy, organizational culture, and HR management practices. The chapter reinforces that inclusive talent management is a shared responsibility, requiring intentional leadership, continuous reflection, and coordinated action to ensure that HR practices are not implemented in pieces but function collectively to strengthen workforce development, organizational effectiveness, and sustainable growth.

Change Management Models

Change management reflects a process flow from "where an organization is" (present) to "where an organization is going" (future). Various models exist to implement organizational change. The sample models referenced below serve as a starting point for implementing changes throughout your organization. These same systems are necessary when adopting talent management practices to expand talent, particularly within the context of recruitment and retention. Several models, such as Lewin's Model of Change, Kotter's Model, and the Malcolm Baldrige, have been transformative in helping many organizations expand their talent supply. Each model of change provides specific guideposts for leadership to navigate change to ensure sustainable outcomes:

- **Lewin's Model of Change:** A three-step change model, unfreezing, changing, and refreezing, where leaders guide and involve employees throughout each phase of the change.
- **Kotter's 8-Step Model:** Provides a systematic approach to managing change by creating urgency, building a team to champion it, developing a clear vision, communicating it broadly, removing barriers, tracking wins, sustaining progress, and integrating it into organizational culture. In construction, engineering, and manufacturing, this could apply to issues such as labor shortages, retention, safety, culture, and upskilling. For example, a manufacturing firm facing high turnover might begin by showing the onboarding of ELL employees, launching a branding initiative, developing an outreach strategy, and piloting an ambassador program for retention.
- **Malcolm Baldrige:** The Malcolm Baldrige National Quality Award (MBNQA) is an award established by the US Congress in 1987 to raise awareness of quality management and recognize US companies that have implemented successful quality management systems. The award is the nation's highest presidential honor for performance excellence. The performance system consists of the following categories: leadership, strategy, customers, workforce operations, results, and measurement, analysis, and knowledge management. Many instances of success have been recognized for construction, manufacturing, and engineering firms (2024, Freese and Nichols Inc., a Texas, privately owned business focused on water supply and wastewater treatment). The website contains a search feature to explore other Baldrige award recipients.[3]

Positive Impacts of HR Strategy

Similar to the Affirmative Action Plan mentioned in Chapter 4, an HR strategy with a Recruitment Plan for outreach to all populations is expected to yield positive outcomes. However, it is essential to determine who will be involved in the recruitment planning and the steps to achieve the goals and objectives. At small firms, the authors would make a different set of recommendations, as the ability to incorporate policies and practices may be limited by the owner, the HR department, or a single manager's capacity to get work done.

HR Action Step: HR Delegation or Outsourcing of HR Strategy

Will you obtain assistance from temporary staffing agencies, Professional Employer Organizations (PEOs), a professional organization that partners with clients to handle administrative employer responsibilities, such as human resources, benefits, and risk management, or other sources to fill positions? If so, what does that look like on a daily, weekly, monthly, or annual basis? If you are working with this type of organization, your goals must be clearly communicated to the organization and implemented accordingly.

Employers Are Talent Builders

We recently surveyed HR representatives to gauge their key challenges in attracting and recruiting top talent. Several respondents noted significant skills gaps between employers' needs and candidates' current skills. Therefore, we recommend that employers view themselves as talent builders to support the upskilling of their current workforce. Training can occur internally, be outsourced to local community colleges, or be achieved through participation in applied apprenticeship programs. Our research, based on case studies of small manufacturing companies, suggests that taking responsibility for staff training fosters loyalty among trainees and enhances their motivation for professional development and advancement.

The Re-evaluation of HR Practices and New Concepts

While some of the action steps and HR practices we discuss here may not be entirely novel, we provide examples of best practices from the field and research to guide efforts to build an inclusive workforce. First, specific HR practices cannot be implemented "in pieces" but must work in unison. The concept of "HR in Pieces" refers to conducting part of an action, typically administrative in nature, as opposed to an HR practice that leads to an outcome that promotes inclusivity. Additionally, these practices should not be acted upon in silos by leadership. We hope you are seeing the relevance of interconnectivity among HR practices and how they inform inclusivity. We refer to this concept as the "HR Collective." HR practices are not conducted in isolation, but rather in sync with the business strategy. The HR Collective works synergistically to guide the development of talent expansion. Similarly, we refer to the HR Collective as the action of HR, which we call the "HR Co-active." According to *Merriam-Webster's Dictionary*, the term *co-active* means acting together in concurrence. It is our experience and opinion that leaders who work in tandem to address HR problems are effective. We need leadership to work cooperatively, continuously, and courageously to support HR practices that strengthen a diverse workforce. Additionally, leadership needs to assume a set of unique responsibilities to ensure HR practices are not abandoned throughout the implementation stages. When this occurs, it erodes trust and accountability within the organization, decreasing morale and potentially contributing to employee turnover. While these phenomena occur in many organizations and do not apply solely to inclusivity, the concepts, when adopted, will strengthen leadership's ability to implement inclusive recruitment and retention practices.

HR in Pieces: This term is used to describe administrative HR practices that occur without a clear linkage to business strategy or inclusive management outcomes.

Example: The company determines that blind hiring will be a practice, then fails to train supervisory-level staff to use the applicant tracking system to "anonymize" applicant materials.

HR Collective: This term is used to describe how the practices should consist of synergistic elements to achieve specific outcomes within the business strategy.

Example: Missteps and restarts occur when leadership attempts to implement a practice but lacks a plan for fully executing it from conception through implementation.

HR Co-active: It requires all leaders to have the following: (1) awareness of the strategic HR practice; (2) knowledge of how to implement it; (3) tools and resources to reinforce it; (4) time and budget to maintain it.

Example: *All levels of leadership participate in HR practice and implementation.*

Example: *Manufacturing Firm—Ask all levels of management and staff to understand and contribute to training on the mission, vision, and core values.*

HR Action Step: Train Leaders on ALL HR Practices

There is a common understanding that all levels should contribute to the design, development, and implementation of HR practices. Despite this, some companies fail to maintain this level of transparency and visibility across their organizations. To address these issues, it is essential to provide all leaders with training on developing an inclusive recruitment strategy. When these three HR practices are cohesively integrated into business practices across all levels, positive changes and impacts on long-term outcomes are possible.

Putting It into Practice

The chapter concludes with actionable steps that support stronger, more intentional recruitment planning to reinforce the importance of clear expectations, structured processes, collaborative input, and intentional communication at every stage of hiring. Each step highlights potential benefits, possible limitations, and the organizational impact when implemented effectively.

Recruitment Strategy: Developing an organization-wide recruitment strategy strengthens alignment across teams and expands access to diverse talent networks such as community partners, educational institutions, professional associations, and internal pipelines. The advantage of this approach is that it broadens visibility and reduces overreliance on a single hiring source. A potential drawback is that it requires sustained coordination and monitoring to remain effective. When implemented well, a comprehensive strategy ensures the organization consistently attracts candidates who match evolving workforce needs and long-term talent goals.

Inclusive Hiring Protocols: Ensuring clear, fair, and accessible hiring materials creates a more welcoming entry point for a wide range of applicants. The benefit of transparent protocols is that they reduce ambiguity and strengthen fairness across the evaluation process. However, if not updated regularly, protocols can become outdated or unintentionally restrictive.

Implementation of inclusive practices results in more consistent screening, improved applicant experiences, and a broader, more qualified candidate pool.

Training on Hiring Practices: Standardized training gives leaders and supervisors a shared understanding of how to recruit, screen, interview, select, and onboard candidates. The advantage is that it increases consistency and reduces personal bias in decision-making. The challenge is that training requires time and follow-through to ensure application across all levels. When executed effectively, equitable implementation of hiring practices leads to smoother onboarding, stronger role alignment, and greater trust in leadership.

Continuous Improvement: Regularly reviewing hiring data, applicant feedback, and new-hire experiences allows leaders to identify patterns, refine processes, and adjust strategies in real time. The benefit of continuous improvement is that it keeps recruitment responsive to organizational needs. A potential limitation is that without dedicated time and ownership, follow-through may lag. When applied consistently, continuous improvement fosters an adaptable, data-informed talent acquisition system that remains competitive and sustainable over time.

Strengthening recruitment requires intentionality, clarity, consistency, and leadership commitment at every level of the organization. When leaders align strategy, values, and practice, they create conditions where strong talent pipelines can grow and sustain the future workforce. As we move forward, the next chapter will build from this foundation by examining how organizations can translate strategic recruitment planning into scalable workforce development practices that prepare individuals for long-term career success.

Notes

1 McKinsey and Company (2023). Diversity Matters Even More: The Case for Holistic Impact. https://www.mckinsey.com/featured-insights/diversity-and-inclusion/diversity-matters-even-more-the-case-for-holistic-impact.
2 Pollack, A., Glasgow, D., Van Bommel, T., Joseph, C., and Yoshino, K. (2025). Risks of Retreat: The Enduring Inclusion Imperative. Catalyst & Meltzer Center for Diversity, Inclusion, and Belonging.
3 NIST (n.d.). Retrieved from https://www.nist.gov/baldrige/award-recipients?year=All&sector=1939016&title=&state=All&field_baldrige_multi_year_value=0

Chapter 6

Community Engagement and Partnership Roles in Recruitment

According to Henry Ford, coming together is a beginning, staying together is progress, and working together is success. Regardless of our religion, race, creed, or background, we need each other to be successful. We must work together to achieve common goals and move forward in the face of changing technological times. If employers want to hire people from all populations, engaging with, among, and throughout the community is crucial.

Community plays an integral part in talent expansion, in both identifying and scaling up talent. In the Talent Expansion Framework (TXF), we address key questions that will enable employers to understand how to engage, partner, and strengthen talent pipelines (see Figure 6.1). By examining the potential applicant pool within the community and by providing a visible presence as an "employer of choice" from a marketing perspective, employers gain deeper insights into community demographics and the skills available in their targeted region. Additionally, a working knowledge of how partnerships can foster connections across educational, industry, and other nonprofit-based support organizations can be beneficial. This chapter will address how to navigate the community engagement process, including specific examples of how partnerships can expand talent.

Identifying Talent in Technical Industries

More importantly, in technical industries, students, adults, and other career transitioners (known as incumbent workers) thrive in hands-on learning environments. Therefore, you may not find candidates for employment in typical programs, such as community colleges and four-year programs. You may find them out in the community doing . . . guess what? Working in technical industries such as construction, engineering, and manufacturing, individuals may work alongside their grandfathers, fathers, or church members, or in other odd jobs.

DOI: 10.4324/9781003515937-7

Figure 6.1 Community Focus of Talent Expansion Framework. Image Credit: Laurel A. Royer (2026)

> Example: *For over 20 years, my husband has operated a small, minority-owned construction firm. When he started in the early 2000s, we did not have as many social media outlets or technologies to assist us with recruitment. On weekends, we would ride by the local hardware store. Inevitably, skilled tradespeople were present and ready to share their expertise and work on day-to-day, week-to-week, and month-to-month jobs. Several of those people demonstrated their skills, and we hired them permanently. Today, with the abundance of qualified talent dwindling, opportunities are available online and at local temporary agencies.*

HR Action Step: Survey the "Proverbial" Land to Find Workers

We are not advocating for hiring someone who is not licensed to perform work safely and to quality specifications. What we are emphasizing is that there is not only interest in technical fields, but people are already doing the work informally for friends, family, and churches. Most notably, if you look at the demographic profile of individuals doing that work, you may find many are immigrants, undocumented, non-White, or from an otherwise marginalized community, including homeless veterans. Why does this matter? We know from community outreach initiatives that those who may be experiencing hardship, addiction, disease, and homelessness may not want to share their story. However, as employers, we need to go where they may be working, learning, and living. Although the individuals we seek are no longer located outside a retail establishment, other communal access points may still exist, including temporary staffing agencies and nonprofit organizations like Goodwill and the Veterans' Administration (VA). We address special populations, and the importance of scouting among the underrepresented and marginalized in your region, in Chapter 7.

Case Study Example: *One manufacturing firm is reaching out to candidates in adjacent industries like retail stores and restaurants to engage with candidates who are making similar or less wages to recruit them to work at their factory. They provide the new hires with training and ongoing professional development.*

Case Study Example: *Another organization is partnering with nonprofits, like those who serve justice-involved individuals to entry level roles.*

As an employer, are you aware of your community partners, community presence, and the populations you serve? As an organization, do you conduct research on your target demographic to better understand and deliver on your customers' wants and needs, with the expectation that the knowledge and information will be converted to sales, outcomes, and long-term sustainability in the marketplace? What we will address in this chapter will require you to ask those same questions, but in reverse. You will conduct inquiries about your target talent pipeline and then take action based on the findings.

The Community Immersion Checklist

For the past 17 years, I (Leressa) have been certified to teach first aid and CPR for the lay responder. My journey with the Red Cross began as a way to fill a need, serving as the "HR department of one" for our family-owned construction company. As part of the Red Cross training, the course curriculum includes valuable checkpoints throughout to ensure the safety of an individual in a community. In the lay responder course, we start with the "3 Cs" for emergency action steps: (1) check the scene, (2) check the person, and (3) care for conditions you may find.

These same action steps provide relevant and valuable context for employers to approach community engagement. Therefore, we aim to delve deeper into this concept within this chapter, referring to it as "*community immersion.*"

When enough people are trained in CPR, the chances of survival increase by 40 percent. Therefore, it is essential to certify as many people as possible. When conducting CPR, it is referred to as performing key steps within the Cardiac Chain of Survival. These action steps are (1) Recognize Signs of Cardiac Emergency, (2) Call 911 or a Cardiac Care Team, (3) Start CPR, 4) Use an Automated External Defibrillator (AED). In this process, each person has a role to fulfill within the Cardiac Chain of Survival. Let's continue to use this example throughout the chapter to address how community engagement can be facilitated as a method of infusing talent in technical industries.

As an employer, HR practitioner, or workforce development professional, if the workforce chain of progress is disrupted, "the system" and the labor force are affected. The work stops, productivity stops, wages stop, and the economy stops. Regarding training, communities are essential; we must work together as a community to create safe jobs and maintain livable wages.

During emergencies, each person plays a pivotal role in ensuring survival. That is why, during an emergency, you call a person's name and say, "You call 911." There is no room for duplication of efforts, no time for missing action steps, or confusion on process or procedure.

We have converted these action steps to a Community Immersion Checklist (CIC) to address any gaps in recruitment trends. This comprehensive checklist enables you to conduct a gap analysis, understanding the community partnership supply versus job seeker demand, which will help fill shortages within a technical industry talent pipeline. The checklist in Table 6.1 introduces the necessity of each component, but further clarity and context will be provided throughout the chapter. The Community Immersion Checklist provides a foundation for understanding how to address the community focus area of the TXF.

Table 6.1 The Community Immersion Checklist (CIC)

- ☐ Search the demographic composition of your local town, city, and regional area to ensure you understand how to locate talent, conduct outreach, attract, recruit, and retain talent.
- ☐ Identify the partners within your community that provide services to special populations and other opportunities to expand talent.
- ☐ Develop an effective employer brand that is well-known to your community.
- ☐ Understand how job seekers are learning about employers in the region (i.e., access to workforce development boards, temporary staffing, traditional job boards, etc.).

Employers, job seekers, educators, and policymakers should approach the workforce system as an economic emergency. When emergencies occur, people mobilize and respond to the event with funding, supplies, helping hands, knowledge, and additional resources. Our recommendations for building a qualified workforce in technical industries, particularly those that drive our US economy, involve identifying best practices for mobilizing the whole community, community leaders, organizations, and partnerships across K–12, two- and four-year colleges, apprenticeships, and other work-based learning agencies. Systems that prepare factory workers, field staff, engineers, and other makers worldwide should be prioritized.

Check the Community to Identify the Talent Pool: Identify and Build Relationships with Community Partners

We recommend creating a table of local, state, and regional for-profit, non-profit, and religious agencies that offer programs to assist employers in attracting and recruiting talent from diverse racial, cultural, and ethnic backgrounds. Table 6.2 can be expanded to serve as a resource guide for connecting with partners in your region. The partnerships created will be mutually beneficial for you as the employer and the respective organizations.

Table 6.2 provides an excerpt from the table generated by ChatGPT for state, federal, and local agencies and job boards in Virginia. Still, a similar table can be developed to assist you in your region.

Table 6.2 Community Agencies and Job Boards Directory

Agency/Platform	*Primary Function*	*Website*
Virginia Career Works Statewide	Statewide employer–job connector by job seekers; workforce development and retention programs.	https://virginiacareerworks.com/
Virginia Registered Apprenticeship (DOL/VA Works)	Help establish Registered Apprenticeships in IT, engineering, and skilled trades.	https://www.doli.virginia.gov/
Virginia Department for Aging and Rehabilitative Services	Provides access to job seekers with disabilities and offers assistive technology services and accommodations.	https://www.dars.virginia.gov
American Job Center/CareerOneStop	National network provides support for recruiting, talent matching, and access to employment resources.	https://www.careeronestop.org/Business Center/Toolkit/

(Continued)

Table 6.2 (Continued)

Agency/Platform	*Primary Function*	*Website*
US DOL Apprenticeship.gov	Employer resources and toolkits for creating or joining Registered Apprenticeship programs.	https://www.apprenticeship.gov
DoD Skill Bridge	Connects employers with transitioning service members through paid internships.	https://skillbridge.osd.mil/industry-employers.htm
DOL Veterans' Employment and Training Service (VETS)	Supports the hiring of veterans and military spouses through various programs.	https://www.dol.gov/agencies/vets/hire
EARN (Employer Assistance and Resource Network)	Helps employers recruit and retain employees with disabilities.	https://askearn.org
JAN (Job Accommodation Network)	Free guidance on workplace accommodations and other employment issues.	https://askjan.org

Check the Partnerships: Identify Organizations Working with Special Populations

- Identify not-for-profits that work with each special population (i.e., veterans, disabilities, justice-involved, immigrants/refugees, and others).
- Seek partnerships with specialty staffing firms.
- Speak at local community events.
- Post jobs at other non-technical spaces to entice candidate job transition (i.e., retail locations, restaurants, grocery stores).

The Need to Work Together

The word *community* refers to specific types of engagement. According to the *Oxford English Dictionary*, it refers to:

1. A group of people living in the same place or having a particular characteristic in common.
2. A feeling of fellowship with others, as a result of sharing common attitudes, interests, and goals.

Where a sense of community exists, common ground, fellowship, and collaboration are more likely to occur, leading to the achievement of goals. When leaders revisit what diversity means to them, it is essential to consider their lived experiences within their community and how diversity was perceived there.

Consider these two profiles from our case study research and historical context.

Profile 1

When we asked a leader why diversity was important to him, he said, "In our community, we were all there to help each other. We came from diverse religions, backgrounds, and races, and spoke various languages, but we prioritized taking care of our people. The other reason diversity is important to me is my mother—her influence."

When we value community and believe that taking care of it is the right thing to do, then our goal extends beyond merely improving diverse outcomes. It becomes a way of doing business, an embedded part of the strategy, tactics, and operations. The example in Profile 1 demonstrates that development not only influences diversity, but it is also the "heart of diversity." If community is the WHY, then community should be an active participant in continuing to move diversity forward in the workplace. Community not only drives diversity through common goals, beliefs, and values, but it is also responsible for achieving it. The leader in Profile 1 reflected upon the community as the "why" and the "how." This is a prominent example of community immersion.

Table 6.3 provides an example of how various small, medium, and large companies facilitate engagement with community partners. Specifically, companies work with justice-involved partners, nonprofits, and local and state governments.

Table 6.3 Examples of Employer Partnerships

Sector	*Company/ Initiative*	*Community Partner(s)*	*Strategy Highlights*
Manufacturing	Talan Products (ACCESS program)	Towards Employment: Precision Metal Forming Association	Reentry-focused recruitment pipeline
Manufacturing	San Antonio Second-Chance Initiative	Manufacturing Institute; Stand Together Trust	Multi-employer, holistic second-chance hiring model
Construction/ Manufacturing	Noujaim Tool Co. Apprenticeships	Local technical high school, community college, state centers	Earn-while-learning trades pipeline
Engineering (Leadership)	Schneider Electric via Specialist Staffing	Specialist Staffing Group	External recruiter to intentionally diversify leadership

While Profile 1 provides context for diversity based on internal characteristics of the leader, the reverse is true when the community is prepared to support the employer's diverse perspectives.

Profile 2

Founded in 1967 by developer James Rouse[1], Columbia was designed to be a model city promoting inclusiveness and equality. It aimed to eliminate racial, economic, and religious segregation by creating a community where people of diverse backgrounds could live, work, and thrive together.

Columbia is divided into ten villages, each with its own schools, shopping centers, recreational facilities, and places of worship, encouraging local engagement and a close-knit feel.

The villages are designed to facilitate interaction and collaboration among residents.

- **Focus on Diversity:** Columbia was one of the first communities planned to embrace diversity as a guiding principle explicitly. Housing was designed to be accessible to people across income levels, with a mix of single-family homes, apartments, and townhouses.
- **Amenities and Culture:** Columbia includes cultural centers, parks, trails, and public spaces to bring people together. Institutions like the Columbia Association organize events and programs that celebrate different cultures and promote community involvement.
- **Recognition:** Columbia is often ranked among the best places to live in the US due to its emphasis on quality of life, inclusivity, and diversity.

Diversity across localities, regions, states, and countries requires a strong commitment to ensure we can move together, grow together, and achieve intended results. Suppose you are serious about establishing diverse talent pipelines in your organization, community, or state. In that case, the first step in prioritizing community engagement is to identify who will be in your sphere of influence.

As practitioners, policymakers, and activists for justice and change, we cannot advocate for a change that we are not willing to embark on as conveners in the field. With that in mind, it is necessary to *investigate your community engagement status*. Understand who you work with in the community for recruitment, collaboration, support, and additional subject matter expertise, as well as engagement.

In this chapter, we explore various types of community partnerships and engagements necessary for attracting and retaining talent. Then, we share relevant best practices and case studies, which can serve as models for how you can alter and strengthen your current interactions with industry, partners, and the broader community to diversify talent pipelines in your area.

First, employers need to recognize the privilege and responsibility they hold for contributing to the economic stability of not only their own firms, but also the communities, surrounding regions, and the US economy more broadly. Equally, employers should be applauded for their efforts to maintain production during challenging times (e.g., during the COVID-19 pandemic), as well as for adapting to the changing technological landscape of "new equipment," learning curves, and rising supply chain costs.

Reflective Prompt:

How are manufacturing firms engaging with local communities?

Reflective Prompt:

How are construction firms ensuring their presence is known in their community?

HR Action Step: Understand the Applicants' Job Search Process

As an organization, what are your typical methods of engaging with prospective candidates? Are you sticking to the usual suspects, such as LinkedIn, online job sites, social media, and word of mouth? It is essential to explore non-traditional engagement methods with special populations that may work in technical industries:

1. Make a list of current recruiting mechanisms.
2. Cast a wider net on technical occupation-specific platforms.

Below is a broad list of examples for occupation-specific platforms you may not be familiar with, but there are likely many others. For example, there are the following construction, manufacturing, and engineering job boards:

a. ConstructionJobs.com
b. iHireConstruction
c. Construction Job Force
d. BuildWitt Jobs (manufacturing/engineering)

Before the COVID-19 pandemic, working in roles within your local community and region was the only option. However, the pandemic has expanded the working capacity of our communities beyond traditional borders. Technology and the future of work have improved access to opportunities, shedding light on new career pathways for diverse populations. For example, enhancing broadband access can unlock new ways of working. These technological transformations contribute to the revitalization and strengthening of rural communities, economic stability, and innovation.

Community colleges and economic development groups are collaborating to revitalize communities by developing new talent and attracting new industries. Our experiences in HR, talent development, and community engagement have given us a new lens through which to consider partnering with traditional and informal groups, such as churches and schools, as well as more formal partnerships, including employer groups.

Building diverse talent pipelines requires a differentiated group of partners working together. Most literature related to workforce development refers to the intersection and interconnection of groups working together as an *"ecosystem," "coalition," or "association."* However, we recommend forming an intentional alliance with like-minded groups. Building diverse organizations does not happen in isolation from the community as a whole. Therefore, all vested parties need to be actively involved in inclusive action. This begins with community. As HR practitioners, we recommend fully immersing yourself in your local community.

Table 6.4 is a compiled list of broad recruiting options for both small and large construction firms, presented in a side-by-side comparison format.

Table 6.4 Recruiting Options for Construction Firms

Category	*Small Firms (10–200 employees)*	*Large Firms (200+ employees)*
Workforce Planning	Simple project-based forecast, skills inventory	Annual workforce demand modeling, HRIS/ATS analytics
Sourcing	Local schools, workforce boards, nonprofits, word of mouth	National pipelines, universities, unions, staffing agencies, and digital campaigns
Apprenticeships	Basic pre-apprenticeship with state support	Registered multi-trade apprenticeships with unions/training partners
Recruiting Tools	Free/low-cost job boards, social media, referrals	Enterprise ATS, LinkedIn Recruiter, and recruitment marketing campaigns
Hiring Process	Two-step process (phone screen + site visit)	Multi-panel interviews, skills assessments, and background checks
Onboarding	Paper forms, buddy/mentor system, starter PPE	Digital portals, formal orientation, KPI tracking, site-level mentoring
Retention	Safety culture, small bonuses, career ladder	ERGs, leadership development, tuition reimbursement, structured promotion tracks
Metrics	Track three KPIs (time-to-hire, 90-day retention, source of hire)	Full HR dashboards (time-to-fill, cost-per-hire, diversity, attrition, engagement)
Compliance	Basic HR compliance, OSHA training records	Full EEO/OFCCP compliance, workforce demographics reporting

Work with the Community

HR practitioners need to have a clear understanding of their communities, as well as how other adjacent not-for-profit groups can offer assistance in outreach and recruitment. As an employer, consider engaging with churches, local schools, and community colleges to promote technical industries and your community work (as noted in items 1–3 below). Additionally, as an employer, build your brand awareness by attending key industry events (e.g., conferences) as noted in items 1–5.

Working with these groups allows your organization to become a trusted advisor in the community. You will have an opportunity to demonstrate your reputation as an "employer of choice," and any new applicants will want to come work with you.

1. **Churches:** Faith communities are valuable and trustworthy resources for engaging with diverse populations, including youth, immigrants, veterans, and other special groups. Churches serve as a useful resource for promoting outreach and awareness of entry-level roles that do not require a degree, certificate, or extensive training. Additionally, churches serve a broad range of age groups, providing potential opportunities to employ both high school students and retirees. Additionally, individuals with disabilities may benefit from a part-time job opportunity. An added benefit of working with the church population is that they may have a strong faith and demonstrate on-time arrival and/or the ability to pass a drug screen.
   One case study conducted by our team found that an SME manufacturer collaborated with local churches to learn about and engage with immigrant populations from three international companies.

2. **Local High Schools:** According to the US Department of Education, Career and Technical Education (CTE) pathways are available in 16 broad career clusters. Small, medium, and large organizations can offer high school students job shadowing or internship opportunities. The career clusters address pathways for entry into professional and technical industries, and technical sectors are emerging as new professions, as noted by "New Careers" in the occupational index offered federally. The following is a snapshot of occupational clusters that fall into STEM:

   - Agriculture, Food, and Natural Resources (i.e., Food Scientist, Veterinarian)
   - Architecture and Construction (i.e., Architect, Construction Manager, Electrician)
   - Manufacturing (i.e., Machinist, Quality Control Inspector, Robotics Technician)

- Science, Technology, Engineering, and Mathematics (STEM) (i.e., Biochemist, Mechanical Engineer)
- Transportation, Distribution, and Logistics (i.e., Truck Driver, Transportation Planner)

3. **Local Community Colleges:** Whether in a small town or a large urban area, it should be a priority to establish a meet-and-greet with professors and explore potential new programs within the community college sector. Possibilities for engagement include:

   - Sponsoring student work-based learning programs
   - Hiring students to assist with work during the summer or breaks
   - Serve on college advisory boards (i.e., assist with curriculum development)

SME Reflections

The message from Brandon Hensley, PhD, Dean of Career and Technical Education at McDowell Technical Community College, illuminates the value of community college within technical industries. In today's labor market, community colleges are the quiet engine room of technical talent:

> As industry partners, we do three things exceptionally well: align, accelerate, and de-risk. We align programs with fundamental job roles through employer-led advisory boards, faculty externships, and competencies that directly translate to the shop floor. We accelerate talent through short, stackable credentials, apprenticeships, and incumbent-worker upskilling that run nights, weekends, and online, so learners and employers don't have to stop production to skill up. We de-risk the pipeline by sharing the cost of training: leveraging public dollars (Perkins, WIOA, state/customized training funds) and philanthropic grants to modernize labs, adopt emerging technologies, and stand up rapid-response cohorts when demand spikes. In short, companies can pause their in-house training departments because community colleges already provide turnkey, standards-based training for virtually every field, from advanced manufacturing and HVAC to health care, IT, and energy.

Just as important, we strengthen the human side of the system. Community college leaders can convene partners, secure sustainable funding, and recruit the right faculty practitioners, with current industry credentials, who can teach safety, quality, culture, and technical skills. We build noncredit-to-credit bridges, enabling employees to earn both a promotion next quarter and a degree the following year. We support learners with tutoring, coaching, and wraparound services that keep completion and retention high, which most companies don't have the capacity to deliver. The result is a durable workforce model: Employers get a measurable return on skill, faculty stay current through industry engagement, and students move into good jobs on faster timelines. That is how community colleges, as true industry partners, expand technical talent at scale and speed.

Authors' Tip #1: Connecting with Minority-Serving Institutions or Colleges

Although we have broadly mentioned community college engagement, it is essential to dedicate intentional time and attention to HSI (Hispanic-Serving Institutions) and HBCU (Historically Black Colleges and Universities), military academies, and other institutions that serve underrepresented populations. Experience with multiple employers and recruiters suggests that accessing representatives from minority-serving institutions, particularly larger ones, can be complicated and time-consuming, often without yielding immediate results or establishing a clear point of contact. Another helpful approach is participating in career fairs or increasing visibility to support in-person connections. After taking this step, contacting the person in charge of recruiting will be less challenging.

There are 107 HBCUs, including 65 four-year institutions and 42 two-year community colleges. Of the 107 institutions, three are closed, and the US Department of Education does not officially recognize them as HBCUs, or they currently lack accreditation. For a full list of HBCUs, visit thehundred-seven.org/hbculist.html.

4. **Attend Local Conferences in Your Technical Industry:** Most professional organizations offer annual conferences to expand certification credits, provide general professional development, or gauge interest in new products or services. If you have a designated community engagement liaison, ask them to register for the event.

5. **Connect with College Professors:** Understand that you, as the employer, are just as much a commodity to the work-based learning equation as the colleges. Most professors welcome the opportunity to get to know you or your representatives.

   - Volunteer to be a guest speaker
   - Join a community college advisor board
   - Ask about assisting with curriculum development

Table 6.5 Local Conferences in Technical Industries

Conference / Event	*Industry Focus*	*Format and Focus*	*Why It's Valuable for Diverse Technical Recruitment*
SHPE National Convention	Engineering (Hispanic professionals)	In-person; includes career fair, technical panels, and leadership development	One of the largest gatherings of Hispanic engineering students and professionals, offering excellent recruiting access.
Society of Women Engineers (SWE) Conference	Engineering (gender diversity)	Global SWE event	Most prominent advocate for women in engineering; excellent access to diverse talent pipelines.
NACE HBCU and Inclusion Summit	Multiple industries, including engineering and tech	In-person summit blending employers and HBCU representatives	Strategic plan for recruiting Black students from HBCUs across technical disciplines.
Manufacturing Institute Workforce Summit	Manufacturing	Annual in-person summit on workforce solutions	Employers connect with diverse workforce solutions, training partners, and talent pipelines.
AGC Construction Workforce and HR Conference	Construction	New HR-focused event, launched in 2025	Tailored to workforce development in construction—ideal for recruiting diverse technical staff.
Manufacturing Institute "Military to Manufacturing" and MFG Day events	Manufacturing	Career fairs linking veterans with manufacturers; webinars for talent outreach	Supports veteran recruitment by adding diversity through engagement with veterans and military-connected individuals.

Case Study 3: *An employer in a rural community offers STEM camps to engage students in new programs. Many students were from underrepresented populations or marginalized communities. This exposure to STEM concepts serves as a precursor for career exploration. This experience is both a benefit to the future pipeline and to adults potentially gaining awareness of a local employer. Additionally, this builds brand awareness, trust, and commitment in the community.*

Case Study 4: *Community college instructors seek guidance from employers and vendors in construction to outfit technology labs in automation, virtual reality, construction, and advanced manufacturing. By engaging with community colleges, employers can provide opportunities to inform the skill sets of the next generation of technical workers in the long term. In the short-term, they gain access to the best-prepared workforce that meets their specific needs.*

HR Action Step: Work with Conveners

Conveners are key agencies or representatives within a community who are responsible for bringing groups together to meet a specific purpose or outcome:

1. **Economic Development:** Collaborate with local economic development agencies. If you are uncertain of how to engage with this group, you can contact your local workforce development board or chamber of commerce. The organizations typically reside at the state level and are overseen by the state chamber and/or local chambers of commerce.
2. **Workforce Development:** Within your state, workforce development boards assist job seekers with job applications, job fairs, hiring options, and free access to job coaching. In my (Leressa) prior work on affirmative action planning within federal contracting, new jobs must always be listed in the workforce development state agency posting, which these agencies administer.
3. **Chamber of Commerce:** Local chambers of commerce offer a platform for networking, sharing best practices, developing innovative solutions, and fostering collaboration within the community. To locate your local chamber of commerce, contact https://www.uschamber.com/co/chambers.

HR Action Step: Work with Nonprofits

Many organizations, such as the Urban League, Goodwill, and Catholic Charities, have workforce development divisions that help community members establish connections to employment and provide job readiness tools. One case study we worked on not only mobilized nonprofits, such as English as a Second Language (ESL) providers, but also integrated them into their training processes. The ESL group provided staff with free after-hours training to enhance their comfort, confidence, and preparedness to engage throughout the organization, where four languages were spoken on the factory floor and during meetings. Additionally, they leveraged partnerships with a justice-involved organization that vetted individuals and provided training for those interested in entering the textile manufacturing field.

HR Action Step: Work with Industry Associations and Credentialing Agencies

Within technical industries, industry-specific associations provide ongoing communications, newsletters, and up-to-date information on how these careers impact and influence the current workforce. Many organizations offer student memberships at discounted rates. By attending or creating recruiting materials for distribution, you can expect increased outreach and awareness of your organization and the services you offer to staff. Some examples include ASEE, Associated General Contractors of America (AGCA) and Associated Builders and Contractors (ABC), and the Society of Black Engineers.

HR Action Step: Work with Student or Staff Alumni (Referrals)

Working with students, especially alums from former internships, apprenticeships, or employees, has been beneficial in various case studies, especially among small businesses. Two case studies within the manufacturing setting identified referrals as their top recruitment tool. Most notably, employers mentioned that those referrals generally not only performed at similar levels but also embodied the organization's culture and standards. While we cannot ignore the fact that referrals can have an adverse effect when not properly managed, they can typically be a strong recruiting tool.

Attracting, recruiting, and retaining talent can be a challenging and cumbersome process. While C-suite individuals can chart the course and develop strategies to ensure the processes are in place, they cannot do it alone. One leader or a cohort of leaders often lacks the bandwidth and foresight to ensure all areas of talent management are in place. Reliance on community partners, such as nonprofits and educational institutions, will serve as a connector to top talent.

Our research indicates that the elements of community that contribute to expanding and unlocking the potential of racially, culturally, and ethnically diverse talent must involve all community members (demographics of the community), business partnerships, company branding, and leadership liaison.

The guiding questions in the community focus within the Talent Expansion Framework signal thought-provoking actions for leadership's consideration. However, these questions are not enough. Leadership must continually engage in evaluative processes to attract, recruit, and retain talent. As skill sets, communities, and industries shift, questions should remain consistent. We recommend leaders meet early and often address the HR management and HR development needs of the organization.

Conclusion

In today's competitive talent landscape, community engagement and strategic partnerships are no longer optional components of recruitment strategy: They are essential pathways to building diverse, skilled workforces that reflect and serve the communities in which organizations operate. As this chapter has demonstrated, successful talent expansion requires employers to move beyond traditional recruitment channels and actively invest in relationships with educational institutions, industry consortia, workforce development organizations, and community-based support networks. By positioning themselves as visible employers of choice within their targeted regions and committing to collaborative talent development initiatives, organizations gain privileged access to untapped talent pools while simultaneously strengthening the economic vitality of the communities they serve. The partnerships and engagement strategies outlined in this chapter provide a roadmap for employers to navigate the complexities of community-based recruitment, from identifying hands-on learning opportunities in technical industries to scaling talent pipelines through sustained, authentic relationships. Ultimately, the Talent Expansion Framework recognizes that talent development is a shared responsibility, and organizations that embrace this collaborative approach will be better positioned not only to meet their immediate hiring needs but to build resilient, future-ready workforces capable of thriving amidst ongoing technological and demographic change. As Henry Ford observed, working together is success, and in the context of modern talent acquisition, this success is measured not just in positions filled but in communities strengthened and opportunities expanded for all.

Putting It into Practice

Using Artificial Intelligence (AI) Prompts

To put community immersion into practice, we offer AI prompts designed to help you make broad-level connections, thereby enhancing your ability to attract, recruit, and retain talent in your specific technical industry.

To use ChatGPT or any other platform, simply put these questions in the dialogue box and press Enter to get a response.

Community Attraction Strategy Prompts for AI

- Identify community and faith-based organizations in my area and develop a branding strategy for my technical industry to attract new employees.
- How can the leadership/CEO and others engage with their local community to share their organization's mission and the skills required?
- What types of speaking opportunities are there in my area for employers to share best practices and position themselves as thought leaders in the region?

Community Recruitment Strategy Prompts for AI

- What community organizations can assist in recruiting [role*] within my state? (Add the role to the sentence to strengthen your search criteria.)
- If you are a job seeker, what are some characteristics you want your employer to offer employees?
- Based on my community demographic in [enter your state here], what organizations can assist with engaging all populations in my organization's job recruitment efforts?

Community Retention Strategy Prompts for AI

- What do former employees in technical industries state as reasons for leaving their employers in my state [or region or local community]?
- What competitive advantages do employers offer in technical industries, and how can my organization strategically implement them across short-, mid-, and long-term strategies?
- What are some practical training, mentoring programs, and professional development activities to strengthen leadership skills for front-line, mid-level, and upper-level supervisors?

Note

1 Stamp, J. (2014, April 23). James W. Rouse's Legacy of Better Living Through Design, Retrieved from: https://www.smithsonianmag.com/history/james-w-rouses-legacy-better-living-through-design-180951187/

Chapter 7

Targeting Special Populations for Recruitment

Recruitment in the manufacturing sector faces several challenges, particularly in attracting and retaining a diverse workforce. Historically, the manufacturing industry has struggled to include a diverse array of demographic groups, resulting in a workforce that does not accurately reflect the population's diversity. The importance of fostering diversity and inclusion within the workforce cannot be overstated, as a more inclusive environment promotes innovation, enhances decision-making, and improves overall business performance. A diverse workforce brings a range of varied perspectives, which are crucial to meeting the complex demands of today's global market. Despite the advantages of diversity, certain demographic groups continue to be underrepresented in manufacturing roles. These groups include women, minorities, veterans, and individuals with disabilities. The underrepresentation of these populations limits the potential talent pool and stifles efforts to address the growing skills gap in manufacturing. Therefore, it is crucial for organizations to develop recruitment strategies that intentionally target these underrepresented groups. By addressing these recruitment disparities, companies can tap into a broader range of talents and perspectives, driving both innovation and productivity.

Why Target Special Populations?

Targeting special populations for recruitment provides numerous benefits, starting with the creation of a more diverse workforce. Diversity is linked to higher levels of creativity and problem-solving, as employees from different backgrounds contribute unique insights and ideas. Additionally, by recruiting from underrepresented groups, manufacturing companies can address the existing skills shortage, as they expand their search for qualified candidates to include individuals who may have been previously overlooked. This strategy not only meets immediate labor needs but also fosters long-term growth and stability by cultivating a workforce

DOI: 10.4324/9781003515937-8

equipped with diverse skills and experiences. Moreover, focusing on special populations can help build an inclusive workplace culture where all employees feel valued and supported. An inclusive environment enhances employee engagement, increases retention, and ultimately contributes to a more harmonious and productive workforce. By making a concerted effort to recruit and retain individuals from diverse backgrounds, manufacturers can ensure that they remain competitive in an evolving global marketplace while contributing to broader societal goals of equity and inclusion.

Understanding the Unique Needs of Special Populations

Women in Manufacturing

Women continue to face significant barriers to entry in the manufacturing industry, many of which stem from deep-seated stereotypes and a workplace culture that has traditionally been male-dominated. These barriers can manifest in the form of gender biases during the hiring process, a lack of female role models in leadership positions, and inflexible work arrangements that make it difficult for women to balance family responsibilities with work. To overcome these challenges, companies must adopt targeted strategies, such as implementing mentorship programs that provide guidance and support to women entering the field, offering flexible work schedules, and fostering an inclusive culture that encourages gender diversity at all levels. Highlighting the success stories of women in manufacturing can also serve as an inspiration for others, demonstrating that career growth and fulfillment are achievable in this sector.

Minorities in Manufacturing

Minority groups in the manufacturing industry face both historical and structural challenges, such as limited access to education and job opportunities, as well as biases that persist in hiring practices. To attract more minority candidates, companies must engage in outreach efforts that are deeply rooted in the communities they aim to serve. This can include partnerships with minority-serving institutions, such as Historically Black Colleges and Universities (HBCUs), as well as targeted recruitment programs designed to increase minority representation. Community engagement is also essential, as building trust with underrepresented groups requires a sustained effort to address the barriers and misconceptions that exist within these communities. Furthermore, organizations must work to ensure that once minority employees are hired, they have access to the same opportunities for advancement and development as their peers.

Veterans in Manufacturing

Veterans bring a unique set of skills to the manufacturing industry, including leadership, discipline, and technical expertise gained from their military service. However, many veterans may not immediately see a clear path from their military experience to a civilian manufacturing role. To bridge this gap, companies must work to align military skills with the specific needs of manufacturing positions, offering training programs that help veterans transition into the industry. The benefits of hiring veterans extend beyond technical skills; they often bring a strong work ethic and the ability to work under pressure, which are invaluable in a manufacturing setting. There are also numerous programs and incentives available, such as tax credits and veteran recruitment initiatives, that can help organizations attract and retain veterans.

SME Reflections: A Military Transition Coach

We spoke to an SME who is a military veteran and coach who helps veterans transition to new roles as civilians. She is a scholar in the field who conducts ongoing research to understand the barriers, support systems, and career development opportunities for veterans transitioning into a new field after service. She helped create a profile of a veteran in transition and shared some of the challenges that exist in real-world settings, not only in technical industries, but across all industries.

1. **Demographic Information**
   - Name (or pseudonym): Janice
   - Age: 34
   - Gender: Female
   - Race/Ethnicity: African American
   - Marital/Family Status: Single
2. **Military Background**
   - Branch of Service: Army, role Transportation, rank E-6
   - Years of Service: 20 years
   - Deployments: Bosnia, Kuwait, Iraq, and Afghanistan
   - Transition to Civilian Life: Transitioned out of the military because she couldn't get promoted. Her retirement was forced.
3. **Civilian Career Transition**
   - Current Employment Status: Employed
   - Industry and Role: Public Sector
   - Education and Training: Bachelor's

4. **Challenges in Transition**
    - Identity Shift: Needed to redefine the civilian job expectations, respect you received in the military because of the rank, versus what you receive when you exit, maintain military bearing (tact and diplomacy), and the level of maturity of civilian peers compared to her years in combat zones and leading others.
    - Employment and Skills Gap: Applied for positions similar to her military role, but she was unable to find meaningful work/underemployed (i.e., low pay, underutilization of her skills and education). She took the first available role until she found permanent and suitable employment. She is now working in a role where she's using her military skills.
    - Mental Health and Well-Being: While she has a service-connected disability, the Veterans' Administration (VA) did not rate her at a level where she should not work. Thus, she needs employment. She needs to have time off to go to VA appointments as needed (the same as a doctor's appointment).
5. **Resilience and Coping Strategies**
    - Support Systems: She had little to no support when she left the military as a single parent. She utilized her network of former service members to secure roles until she landed her current job.
6. **Unique Perspectives and Insights**
    - Military Values in Civilian Life: Values like discipline, teamwork, leadership, resilience, work ethic, and dependability.
    - Personal Reflections: "Give veterans a chance, do not stereotype us. We want to be able to do meaningful work and know our work makes a difference. You will get someone who is going to be on time, respectful, loyal, has a sense of duty, and is a hard worker."

Justice-Involved

Many organizations are prioritizing this population to meet talent shortages in construction, manufacturing, and engineering. We will highlight several resources to build, strengthen, and sustain programming if your organization is considering outreach to this population.

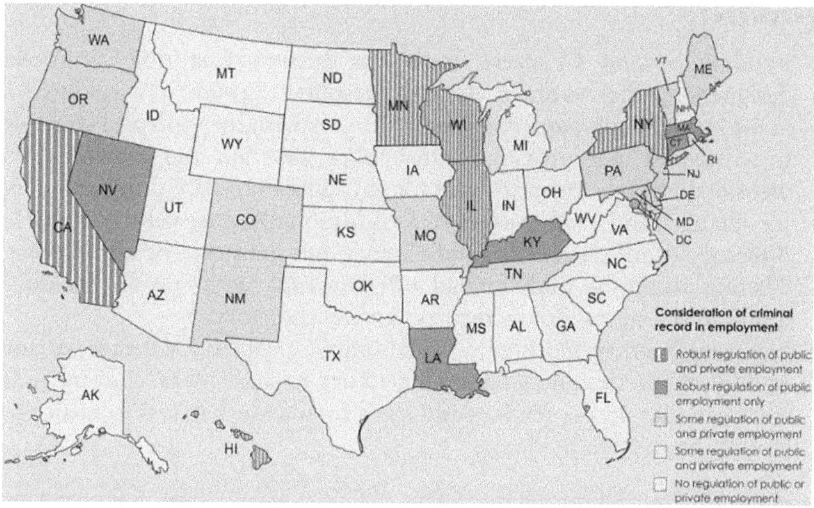

Figure 7.1 Map of US States: Consideration of Criminal Record

Image Source: Center for Criminal Justice Research & Policy (CCJRC) Staff (2022, February 25). *Fair Chance Employment and Occupational Licensure: A National Survey*. CCJRC. See https://niccc.nationalreentryresourcecenter.org/resources/collateral-consequences-resource-center

However, before we can think about hiring in technical industries, we found that many states still have policies regarding criminal records. A report published by a community college resource center provides the color-coded map and ranking of states shown in Figure 7.1. Equally, the state is ranked on a letter grade scale across eight distinct areas. Only a small number of states received high scores in the employment category, and the Center for Criminal Justice Research findings highlight how limited strong fair-chance employment protections remain nationwide. This pattern underscores the unevenness of state-level approaches to regulating the use of criminal records in hiring and the continuing gaps in policy safeguards for justice-involved individuals. Together, these results suggest that robust employment protections are still the exception rather than the norm, leaving substantial room for improvement across most states. Employers often have access to a range of supports that can strengthen efforts to engage justice-involved individuals. These supports may include tax incentives, bonding programs, or formal partnerships with workforce agencies, community colleges, reentry organizations, and other community-based providers. Together, these mechanisms create additional pathways for employers to conduct outreach, reduce perceived hiring risks, and build more inclusive employment practices.

Resources

- Building Second Chances: Tools for Reentry Coalition,[1] a toolkit designed by the National Reentry Resource Center as a resource to assist local, county, and community leaders with the tools and strategies to participate in improving reentry policy, practice, and outcomes. The website addresses key principles for engaging in reentry programs, tools for change, and further resources. Additionally, the website curates a directory of all current Second Chance Act grantees for all 50 states. There is an option to download a PDF of each state's profile, including a link to the states' online reentry services directory.
- National Reentry Workforce Collaborative (NRWC)[2] leverages a community of practice and a national network to share ideas, convene practitioners, and access services and tools to address barriers to justice for justice-involved individuals.

SME Reflection: A Success Story

A formerly incarcerated individual, who has become a successful entrepreneur, shared his story of overcoming extraordinary obstacles to transition from a construction laborer to a construction contractor, working in residential, commercial, and government spaces. We invite you to review some excerpts from a letter in which he tells his story in his own words. The lived experiences of our workforce are meaningful, motivating, and necessary to enact change. We are grateful to share the story to showcase how opportunity, access, and motivation transform job quality and lifestyles.

The Individual and Background

My name is Kevin Blount, the owner of SAFECO Inc., and I identify as African American. I was born and raised in what could, in retrospect, be seen as a troubled childhood. I spent time with both my maternal and paternal grandparents, as I was often in trouble in my home or neighborhood. By the time I was 16, I had joined the thriving enterprise of my neighborhood, crime. I am responsible for my decisions, even for those I made at 16. It was not as if I didn't know it was wrong; I, like many in my neighborhood, just thought I wouldn't get caught. I graduated from high school, somehow, and had nowhere to go, a felony on my record, no college opportunities, and not even the military would accept me with my criminal history.

The Job Search Post-Justice Involvement

I went business to business, looking for something, something that would help put my life on the right track. A local business owner said to me, "You have no experience, and I don't know if I can trust you with anything, but if you are willing to work, I will give you a chance." I took the job, cleaning up behind the construction crews and whatever odd jobs that came up. It was little to no pay, but it was honest pay for honest work. After a period of time, I was given more responsibilities and slowly started making a few more dollars.

Apprenticeship Opportunity

While still working for the construction firm, I applied to the apprenticeship program at the Local Carpenters' Union in 2005. Because of my lack of formal education beyond a high school diploma, they felt I wasn't a good candidate. After their statement that I was not a good candidate, I asked if I could reapply after taking a few classes at the local community college. Their reply was "I just don't think this is a good fit for people like you." I asked the gentleman directly what he meant by "a person like me," and he answered, "You don't look like the type of young man we want to represent the union." After that, I pulled the head person to the side and candidly asked why, and he looked me directly in my eyes and said, "Typically, young black kids don't do well with the school portion of the apprenticeship." The apprenticeship was my only option to increase my pay during that season of my life.

Determination after Rejection

After being rejected from the carpenters' apprenticeship program, I worked harder, learned about construction, and aspired to become an owner. I absorbed as much as I could, worked across all areas of the business, and started taking on small jobs on the side using the knowledge I had gained. I wanted to go back to school and get a formal education in construction management, but it wasn't in the cards; I didn't have the family structure or the money to do so.

I was determined to overcome my past. I applied for a Virginia contractor's license and began looking for work aligned with the skills I had gained during my on-the-job training. I knew it would not be easy. During the application process, I had to appear before a review board, in large part due to my past felony convictions. It was a tough sell; I didn't have the financial backing or the relevant experience, but I was determined. I ultimately got the license, and I felt as if the doors of opportunity had finally opened.

Mr. Blount would go on to endure many setbacks. Overcoming negative comments and a lack of opportunity. Despite many program representatives citing a lack of experience and financial backing, he persevered by leveraging loans from family and friends.

Persons with a Disability in Manufacturing

For individuals with disabilities, the key challenge in entering the manufacturing workforce is often related to accessibility. Companies must take steps to create work environments that accommodate a wide range of physical and cognitive abilities. This includes implementing assistive technologies that enable individuals with disabilities to perform tasks effectively and ensuring that facilities are physically accessible. Stories of companies that have successfully integrated individuals with disabilities demonstrate that when these individuals are given the right tools and support, they can make significant contributions to an organization's productivity and innovation.

Tailored Recruitment Strategies

To ensure targeted, effective outreach to all candidates, employers should be specific about how they tailor messages to demonstrate their intent to serve all populations. Some examples include outreach to target veteran populations using common veteran terms like "military occupational skills" (MOS) or translating compensation levels to military bandings like E4, which stands for "fourth-level enlisted pay grade." CareerOneStop, sponsored by the US Department of Labor, promotes a veterans' job matcher to find civilian careers to be a good match for military skills.

Resources

- **O*NET Online:** A database that contains information on occupations and examples of job descriptions. Review this site for examples of how manufacturing, construction, and engineering job descriptions.[3]
- **CareerOneStop:** A resources for career exploration and training for jobseekers[4]
- **My Next Move:** To learn more about veteran military skills and military occupational skills (MOS), review this site to gain a perspective on how job duties and skills may transfer within military classifications.[5]

Developing Targeted Messaging

To effectively attract underrepresented populations, companies must craft job descriptions and recruitment materials that are both inclusive and appealing. This means avoiding language that might unintentionally exclude certain groups and focusing on the values and opportunities that resonate with them. For example, women may be more attracted to manufacturing roles that emphasize career growth, mentorship, and flexible working conditions. Similarly, veterans may appreciate messaging that highlights the alignment between their military skills and the manufacturing industry's needs. Addressing concerns or misconceptions about the industry, such as the perception of manufacturing as a low-tech or physically demanding field, can help break down barriers and make the industry more attractive to diverse talent.

HR Action Step: Write a Compelling Job Description for Special Populations

[Company Name] prides itself on fostering a supportive, collaborative, and growth-oriented workplace. Our manufacturing facility is not just a place to work; it is where innovation meets dedication. Employees here enjoy an environment that's both high-performing and highly supportive, where everyone from line operators to senior engineers work together with respect, transparency, and a shared drive to achieve excellence.

HR Action Step: Ensure That the Marketing Materials Are Accessible

Ensure your marketing materials, especially your website and social media content, are written and designed in an accessible way, using Universal Design for Learning (UDL) principles that help all viewers engage with your information. This includes offering content in multiple formats such as readable text, infographics, and short captioned videos, providing alternative text for images and graphics, and using plain, culturally inclusive language. It may also be helpful to use colors from the color-blind palettes, such as those found at "Coloring for Colorblindness" by David Nichols to ensure viewers can visualize key distinctions, interpret charts, or graphics accurately, to more fully engage with your materials regardless of their color perception.[6] On social media, UDL principles may include adding alt-text to images (captions that describe visual images for those who cannot see them) and using camel case in hashtags, such as #CareerTraining instead of #careertraining. Using CamelCase in hashtags improves the decoding of long text strings, enhances accessibility for individuals with dyslexia, and allows screen readers to accurately enunciate words instead of mispronouncing continuous text. Also, add captions and transcripts to accompany video posts, and avoid text-heavy graphics that screen readers cannot interpret. Clear layouts, high color contrast, mobile-friendly formatting, and keyboard-accessible elements all contribute to a more inclusive experience for diverse audiences.

Utilizing Digital Recruitment Tools

In today's digital age, companies can leverage online platforms and social media to reach a broader audience. Social media campaigns targeting specific populations, such as women or veterans, can help raise awareness of job opportunities in the manufacturing sector. Additionally, online job boards that cater to underrepresented groups provide a direct way to connect with diverse talent. Virtual job fairs and recruitment events, which have become more common during the pandemic, also offer a cost-effective way to engage with potential candidates from a diverse range of backgrounds.

Building Partnerships and Collaborations

Building strong partnerships with educational institutions, community organizations, and advocacy groups is crucial for long-term success in recruiting diverse talent. Collaborating with trade schools and community colleges can establish a pipeline of skilled workers, while forming partnerships with nonprofit and advocacy organizations can help companies reach underrepresented populations. Developing apprenticeships and internship programs tailored to specific populations enables companies to offer hands-on experience, which can lead to full-time employment while promoting a more inclusive workplace.

Overcoming Common Barriers to Recruitment

Addressing Bias in the Hiring Process

Implicit biases, whether conscious or unconscious, can hinder efforts to create a diverse workforce. To counter this, companies should provide implicit bias training to hiring managers and implement blind recruitment techniques, such as removing names and demographic information from résumés. Structured interviews and standardized assessments can also help reduce bias by ensuring that all candidates are evaluated based on the same criteria, leading to a fairer and more objective hiring process.

Creating an Inclusive Work Environment

An inclusive work environment is essential not just for recruiting special populations but for retaining them. Employee Resource Groups (ERGs) and affinity networks can provide underrepresented employees with a sense of belonging and support. Mentorship and sponsorship programs tailored to the needs of special populations help foster career development and provide the guidance necessary for advancement. Additionally, retention strategies must go beyond recruitment to ensure that all employees feel valued and have access to opportunities for growth and development.

Providing Adequate Training and Support

Offering onboarding programs tailored to the specific needs of special populations is crucial for ensuring a seamless transition into the workplace. Ongoing professional development opportunities, such as training and leadership development programs, enable underrepresented employees to build the skills necessary for career advancement. By investing in the continuous development of diverse talent, companies can create a pipeline of future leaders from within their workforce.

Case Study—Industry Success Stories: *Several companies in the manufacturing sector have successfully implemented recruitment strategies targeting specific populations. These case studies illustrate how targeted approaches can yield positive results in attracting and retaining diverse talent. For instance, a company that implemented a mentorship program for women in manufacturing experienced a notable rise in female hires and retention rates. Analysis of these strategies shows that the key to success lies in understanding the unique needs of different groups and creating tailored solutions that address those needs.*

Benchmarking Best Practices

To measure the success of diversity recruitment efforts, companies must establish key performance indicators (KPIs). These may include metrics such as the percentage of new hires from underrepresented groups, retention rates, and the number of promotions within these groups. Continuous improvement is essential, and companies should seek feedback from employees to refine and enhance their recruitment strategies over time.

The Future of Targeted Recruitment

As technology continues to evolve, it will play an increasingly important role in recruitment. AI-driven recruitment platforms can help match candidates from special populations with roles that align with their skills and experiences. Additionally, data analytics can be used to track recruitment outcomes and identify areas for improvement, enabling companies to fine-tune their strategies. Government programs and initiatives aimed at promoting diversity in the workforce can provide valuable support for companies seeking to recruit special populations. Compliance with equal employment opportunity (EEO) regulations is not only a legal requirement but also a key component of building an inclusive workplace. As the demographics of the workforce continue to shift, companies must be prepared to adapt their workplace cultures to accommodate diverse teams. This includes addressing potential challenges, such as generational differences and cultural diversity, while also embracing the opportunities that a diverse workforce brings.

Conclusion

In conclusion, targeting special populations for recruitment is not only a moral and social imperative but also a business necessity in today's competitive landscape. By developing tailored, inclusive recruitment strategies and fostering a supportive work environment, companies can unlock the full potential of a diverse workforce. The long-term benefits of these efforts include greater innovation, improved performance, and a more resilient workforce. Leaders in the manufacturing industry must take proactive steps to prioritize diversity and inclusion in their recruitment efforts, ensuring the success and sustainability of their organizations for the future.

Putting It into Practice

Self-Assessment of Bias and Leadership Style: Reflect on your own biases and how they may influence your leadership and recruitment practices. Commit to ongoing personal development in this area, including participating in bias training and seeking feedback from peers and team members.

Set Clear Diversity Goals: Define specific, measurable diversity goals for your organization's recruitment efforts. Align these goals with broader business objectives to ensure that diversity is prioritized as a key aspect of organizational growth and development.

Develop Targeted Recruitment Campaigns: Create recruitment campaigns tailored to attract specific populations, including women, minorities, veterans, and individuals with disabilities. Ensure that messaging resonates with these groups and addresses any misconceptions about manufacturing roles.

Partner with Community Organizations and Educational Institutions: Build relationships with trade schools, colleges, and community organizations that serve underrepresented groups. Develop apprenticeship and internship programs to provide opportunities for skill development and career entry.

Review and Revise Job Descriptions: Audit your company's job descriptions to ensure they are inclusive and free from gendered or exclusionary language. Focus on skills and qualifications rather than rigid requirements that may discourage applicants from special populations.

Implement Bias-Free Hiring Practices: Introduce structured interviews, standardized assessments, and blind recruitment techniques to reduce bias in the hiring process. Provide hiring managers with bias training to ensure fair evaluation of all candidates.

Create and Support ERGs: Encourage the formation of ERGs or affinity groups for underrepresented populations within your organization. Provide resources and support to these groups to foster a sense of community and belonging.

Offer Flexible Work Arrangements and Support Services: Develop flexible work policies that accommodate the diverse needs of various populations, including parents, veterans, and individuals with disabilities. This may include offering part-time roles, remote work options, or onsite support services.

Provide Mentorship and Sponsorship Opportunities: Establish formal mentorship and sponsorship programs to support underrepresented employees in advancing their careers within your organization. Pair them with experienced leaders who can offer guidance and advocate for their professional development.

Track and Measure Progress: Use data analytics to monitor the effectiveness of your diversity recruitment efforts. Track key metrics, including the number of hires from underrepresented groups, retention rates, and employee satisfaction. Use this data to make ongoing improvements.

Create an Inclusive Onboarding Process: Design onboarding programs that are sensitive to the needs of special populations. Ensure that new hires feel welcomed, supported, and integrated into the company culture from the start.

Foster an Inclusive Workplace Culture: Commit to building a workplace culture that values diversity and inclusion. Regularly engage employees in discussions around inclusion, provide training, and ensure that your company policies reflect a commitment to equity and respect for all.

Leverage Assistive Technologies: Invest in assistive technologies and accessible workspaces to ensure that individuals with disabilities can thrive in your organization. Regularly assess the physical and digital accessibility of your facilities and tools to ensure they meet the needs of all users.

Utilize Technology for Recruitment: Leverage AI-driven recruitment platforms and data analytics to enhance your ability to identify and attract candidates from special populations. Use these tools to minimize bias and improve decision-making in the recruitment process.

Advocate for Policy Changes: Stay informed about and advocate for policies that promote diversity and inclusion, both within your organization and at the legislative level. Ensure your company is compliant with EEO regulations and is actively working to support diversity in all areas.

Notes

1 National Reentry Resource Center (n.d.). Building Second Chances: Tools for Local Reentry. https://nationalreentryresourcecenter.org/sites/default/files/inline-files/buildingSecondChancesReentryToolkit_508.pdf
2 NRWC (n.d.). Retrieved from https://thenrwc.org/our-approach/
3 O*NET OnLine (n.d.). Retrieved from http://www.onetonline.org/
4 CareerOneStop (n.d.), Retrieved from https://www.careeronestop.org/Toolkit/Jobs/match-veteran-jobs.aspx
5 My Next Move (n.d.). Retrieved from https://www.mynextmove.org/vets/
6 Nichols, D. (n.d.). "Coloring for Colorblindness". https://davidmathlogic.com/colorblind/#%23D81B60-%231E88E5-%23FFC107-%23004D40

Chapter 8

HR Development Practices: Training Programs for Retention

This chapter will primarily focus on training and learning development opportunities, also known as human resource development (HRD), to prepare for skill set changes in technical industries. However, let us explain how this association with training is addressed as "tactical," including its origins and why we believe it is a valuable label that requires proactive and consistent attention.

Initially, the concept of tactical HR practices was part of a conceptual framework developed by professors from Australia Jie Shen, Ashok Chanda, Brian D'Netto and Manjit Monga, to address a "framework of HR diversity management."[1] While their framework addresses other training areas, including staffing, training development, appraisals, and wages, we will address different concepts as part of the diversity management process. Leressa Suber's dissertation offers theoretical, real-life, practical case studies that address this topic.[2]

Within the Talent Expansion Framework (TXF), we zoomed in on HR development aspects to identify how training can influence the design, development, and advancement of technical talent. To promote effective HRD practices, training for leadership and staff is paramount. As technology evolves, accessible training, mobility, and upskilling will help maintain a competitive advantage. Figure 8.1 provides organizational questions to help leaders model, maintain, and monitor equitable training across the organization.

Training as a Tactical Solution

According to *Merriam-Webster's Dictionary*, "tactical" refers to actions or strategies designed to achieve specific, immediate objectives. While the term is often associated with military contexts, its broader application centers on how deliberate actions are used to navigate complex environments and produce desired outcomes. In the context of education and

DOI: 10.4324/9781003515937-9

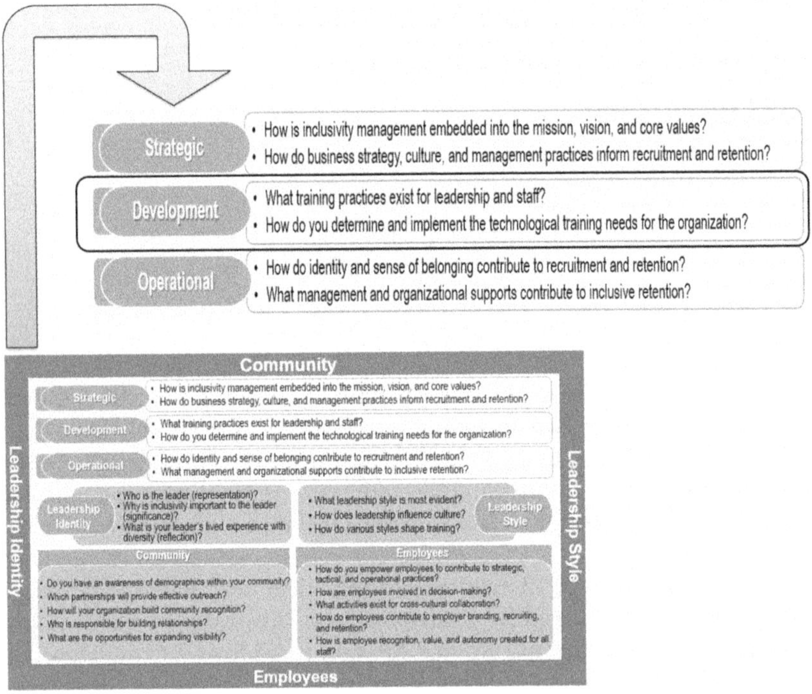

Figure 8.1 Development Focus of the Talent Expansion Framework. Image Credit: Laurel A. Royer (2026)

training, we conceptualize training as a tactical approach to retention and performance improvement across multiple fields. This framing emphasizes the intentional design and deployment of strategies that respond to specific conditions, learner needs, and organizational goals. From this perspective, key questions emerge: (1) What is the context in which training occurs? (2) What conditions shape learning and performance? (3) Who or what influences outcomes? and (4) What tools, strategies, or resources are being leveraged to achieve success?

This chapter will touch upon the answers to these questions across industries. However, broadly, we can simplify it as a competitive field (domestic vs foreign), a production field (what to produce), and a people field (talent). For example, in technical industries such as manufacturing, competition exists for quality production, people, and performance. Within the US, we are lagging behind in both manufacturing processes and skill development. Within construction, new materials are being developed to address alternative supply chain issues and technologies, such as drones acting as co-workers in the field. In engineering, the field is so expansive, from life science to mechanical and industrial to civil, that the talent needed to support STEM fields is massive. Training will impact talent in how we compete in all technical areas as automation moves forward.

A second definition of "tactical," according to *Merriam-Webster's*, refers to "planning or maneuvering to accomplish a purpose." In organizational contexts, this distinction is critical. C-suite leaders and organizational decision-makers must not only define a clear purpose but also understand how that purpose will be achieved in practice. While this definition aligns with strategic human resource management (HRM) through its emphasis on purpose, we argue that strategic HRM defines the purpose, whereas tactical human resource development (HRD) operationalizes it. In this way, HRD provides the concrete actions, interventions, and learning strategies that translate strategic intent into measurable outcomes.

Several internal and external factors are known to influence the need for new training. Examples of training problems identified in technical industries include poor performance, dips in productivity, and high turnover.

Our SME experiences affirm that training aspects of technical industries are reliant on and enabled by significant key indicators. When these indicators are present, they act as levers for why we are "maneuvering" for purpose and *"signal a need for training."*

Industry Expanded: Accommodate the New

When industries expand, sometimes training is needed to shift to a new skill/trade or specialty to achieve the company's purpose.

Assessment Question: What has changed in the current state of industry, market, economy, or policy that's driving the training?

Example: Electric vehicle production increased, and new technicians are needed.

Industry Changed: Abide by the "Who"

When an industry or governing body changes the rules or regulations, upskilling and training are required to align with new standards. Organizations must also remain aware of their political, legal, and compliance obligations.

Assessment Question: What has changed in industry standards, as noted by specific training clusters (see resources below), industry compliance training requirements like Industry Standard Operations ISO practices, or cybersecurity compliance, require additional training of leaders and HR providers.

Example: Within manufacturing, the introduction of ISO, or Industry Standard Operations or specific Informational Technology Training to ensure operations run smoothly.

Industry Composition Impacted: Invite Every You

As a TXF for attracting all candidates to technical industries, the talent pool should be inclusive of every "you." Borrowing from the Army's former marketing statement, "Be All You Can Be," the draw is that every individual can achieve their purpose. As we seek to diversify technical industries, training levels the field for all genders, races, ethnicities, and sexual orientations to envision themselves in construction, manufacturing, and engineering industries.

> ***HR Action Step: Respond to Subject Matter Expert Signals for Training***
>
> Signals for training allow HR practitioners to assess learning. When developing training, training needs assessments (TNAs) are often performed to determine a starting point. A needs assessment is a process for identifying gaps between current performance and desired outcomes. Figure 8.2 provides context for when, why, and how training assessments are needed. Leadership, HR management, learning and development specialists, and other key contributors to staff development should gather consensus to ensure training is needed, meets organizational needs, and is implemented effectively.

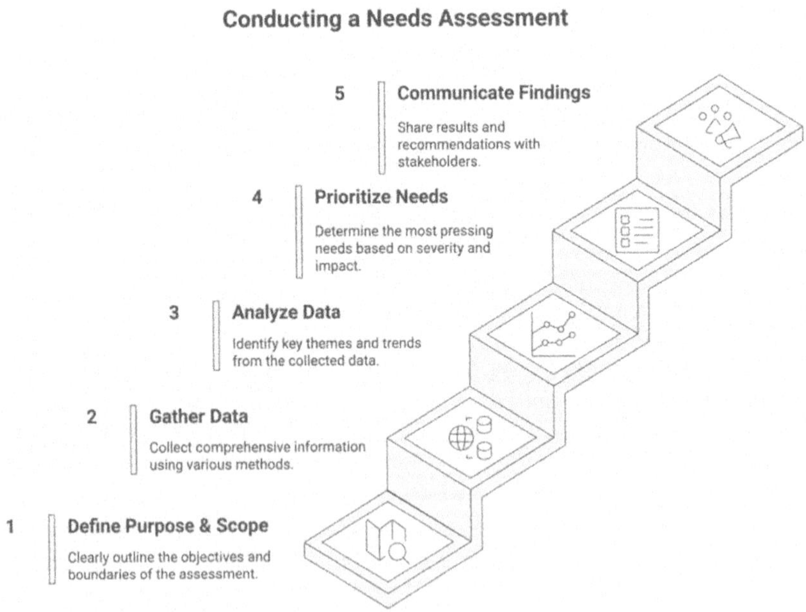

Figure 8.2 Conducting a Needs Assessment. Image Credit: Laurel A. Royer (2026)

The needs assessment process is best understood as a systematic and sequential set of activities that build toward informed decision-making. As shown in Figure 8.2, the process begins by establishing a clear purpose and scope, followed by the deliberate collection and analysis of relevant data. These steps provide the evidentiary foundation for determining the relative importance of identified needs and concluding with the communication of findings to appropriate stakeholders. Presenting the process as a staged progression underscores that each phase is interdependent; the strength of subsequent decisions relies on the rigor and clarity of the earlier steps. This visual representation offers readers a concise overview of the workflow and highlights the intentional structure underlying effective needs assessment practice.

The remaining portion of this chapter will provide in-depth training and development mechanisms for diversifying the technical workforce. Since our expertise is at the intersection of scholarly and practical knowledge, we will provide details on technical workforce ecosystems. Although all organizations need to focus on training, we believe the future talent pipeline of technical industries will undergo the most significant changes through automation and generative artificial intelligence. Therefore, we hope this chapter is the impetus for uplifting, enhancing, and reimagining your learning culture. Our recommendations offer training for leadership and current staff, and opportunities for future consideration in the AI space. The HR collective is needed to ensure effective change management and a smooth transition to automation and technology.

Talent Shortages

Across all technical industries, the labor market is fighting for top talent. Shortages post-COVID continue to impact workforces' ability to meet global competitive advantage. We selected the top three technical areas—construction, manufacturing, and engineering—because they are the foundation of the US economy. The Boston Consulting Group completed an analysis on engineering shortages in its report "The US Needs More Engineers. What's the Solution?" and determined talent shortages are approaching 400,000 workers annually.[3] According to the Associated Builders and Contractors, the construction industry must recruit approximately 501,000 workers, in addition to current hiring numbers in 2024, to meet labor needs.[4] The National Association of Manufacturers reports that talent shortages are more than triple those of construction, with the potential for 2.1 million vacancies in the current workforce.[5]

Talent Tug of War

Since McKinsey proclaimed the US's war for talent in 1998, and "the great resignation" was coined by Anthony Klotz, a psychologist and professor at Texas A&M University, there has been a mighty tug of war between talent and employers in the job market. Employers and recruiters often take turns ghosting or accepting hiring roles or candidates, only to renege on offers and acceptances. As automation takes over technical industries, clarity and specificity on recruitment and retention practices are critical. Prioritizing the diversification and expansion of talent pools in manufacturing, construction, and engineering is crucial for achieving a global competitive advantage and innovative practices. Employers, policymakers, practitioners, and job seekers must all take responsibility for shaping how roles are filled in the future. As AI and automation continue to advance, we will interact with our new co-workers, robots, and other technologies. Their introduction to the field will place greater strain on the "human aspects" of work. We will address how our research (case studies, interviews, focus groups) informs how training is a catalyst for success in technical industries, and share tips and strategies for building equitable and inclusive training programs that benefit the bottom line and employee belonging.

Technical Industry Composition + Treatment

As we said above, in training within HRD a central question to ask is "What are the conditions in the field?" To answer this question, we will provide an overview of the talent working in the field, along with their perceptions and treatment within the industry.

The talent demographic is predominantly White males between the ages of 24 and 45, with education ranging from certificates to bachelor's degrees. Within technical industries (construction, manufacturing), immigrant workers, and underrepresented minorities (African American/Black, Asian Pacific Islander, and Native American) make up less than 11 percent of the workforce. However, Hispanics account for the largest share of the construction industry, at 30 percent.[6] Despite the variations in representation across technical industries, most roles are not at the management level and have room for continued talent expansion. The demographic composition of the manufacturing talent pipeline is disproportionate in some states, with the White population overrepresented. For example, while 80 percent of the US manufacturing workforce is White,[7] only 68 percent of the North Carolina adult working population is White.[8]

To ensure a racially diverse workforce and influence the talent pipeline, additional equitable training and outreach to underrepresented groups (see Chapter 7) are required to ensure their inclusion in opportunities in these fields. While the focus of this book is not to address and solve the systematic barriers that have prevented these groups from entering or advancing in these fields, it is necessary to emphasize their existence. Many women have been overlooked, excluded, and mistreated in technical fields, leading to their departure from them. For example, the language used in technical settings has been described by women as foul, degrading, demoralizing, and insensitive. They have described behaviors they encountered in technical settings, such as insulting, assaulting, and revolting. Prior to the 1960s, it was rare to see a woman working in a male-dominated industry such as construction. Today, more research is being conducted on how to improve women's persistence in the field, with evidence suggesting women's resilience, career interests, and self-efficacy are factors. Despite progress in gender diversity within technical industries, further work is required to enhance equity. The reputations of these industries must be transformed by unlearning harmful behaviors and relearning to respect and accept each other for our differences and commonalities.

Business Case for Training

According to the Associated Builders and Contractors Workforce Development Survey, construction companies are spending 7.5 percent of payroll on education.[9] Using data from the FMI-ABC 2024 Workforce Development Survey, firms collectively invested $1.6 billion in workforce development in 2023, supporting training and professional development efforts to cultivate new talent.

Formal Training (External)

There has been considerable attention given to formal construction, engineering, and manufacturing programs. Federal programs such as the Occupational Safety and Health Association (OSHA), American Society for Engineering Education (ASEE), and the National Association of Manufacturers (NAM) seek to ensure professional development is accessible and attainable. With the emphasis on diversifying industries, these organizations have been at the forefront of technical education. Opportunities for continued outreach to fill talent shortages should be considered for small, medium, and large corporations.

HR Action Step: Follow Public Agencies and Funding Allocations

Public agencies provide context about new career pathways and talent development to gain insights into the latest trends, the current state of the industries, and gaps in advancing the field. Organizations such as the National Science Foundation (NSF) fund new programs that typically focus on emerging technologies needed to advance the technical workforce. As HR practitioners and employers, following these associations and funding allocations/priorities will enable you to forecast future career pathways and role changes on the horizon. Although organizations like Harvard Business Review offer white papers and reports on future roles by 2030, these assumptions are rapidly evolving as political, economic, and societal environments change. To mitigate funding stream shortages, continue to monitor funder priorities to determine where allocations will be prioritized across industries. Prior to political shifts, examples included the NSF and the National Institute of Standards and Technology (NIST), which fund Manufacturing Extension Partnerships, domestically serving manufacturers across all 50 states within the US. Additionally, this action step aligns with our previous recommendation about signaling training; when an industry regulation or policy changes, funding agencies, private foundations, and other policy-enabled think-tanks can assist with understanding what new requirements exist. More importantly, each of these groups pays special attention to ensuring access for underrepresented minorities and special populations.

HR Action Step: Connect with Education Institutions (Local-State-National)

Community colleges and four-year universities are producing the most diverse talent across the country. These institutions are not only a source of talent but also partners to assist in your next hiring opportunity. As an HR practitioner and employer, your pain points with daily projects are a driving factor for new curricula across the country. Therefore, your input on the new industry curriculum is vital for emerging technological change and advancement. Community college presidents, deans, professors, adjunct faculty, and students all require guidance on the specific knowledge and skills students should acquire to enter the field. Our work has demonstrated that positive interactions occur among institutions and employers through the following connections:

1. **Connect with Minority-Serving Institutions:** Many employers seek opportunities to engage with these (two- and four-year institutions).
2. **Serve on College Advisory Boards:** Contact local community college system or the department head of manufacturing, engineering, construction.
3. **Contribute to Curriculum Development:** Participate in the curriculum development and revision process by assisting with a job task analysis to inform the curriculum. A job task analysis is a systematic process of determining a detailed job description, categorized by performance domains and tasks that define what will be required in the job.

Formal In-House Training (Internal)

Returning to the battlefield example, where is the battle located? Within technical industries, the internal work is literally done in a field, which may be a work site (construction), factory (manufacturing), or testing lab (engineering). Therefore, the training ground for these types of industries requires more flexible and practical applications. Most organizations, large and small, can offer their own customized training applications specific to the needs of the organization or the customers. We highlight some options for building formal internal programs that have been effective in small, medium, and large business cases. We will address the specific emphasis on diversity within each training practice. Additional resources for developing these types of programs will be mentioned and summarized in the action steps at the end of the chapter.

Apprenticeship Programs (External)

Apprenticeship programs are valuable tools for providing on-the-job training (OJT) to individuals in technical fields. As automation continues to gain popularity, these training models are not standardized and exhibit significant variation in curriculum, employer outreach, and participant perceptions. As previously mentioned, global competition is ongoing. Who are the competitors on the workforce battlefield? Specifically, countries such as Spain, the United Kingdom, Singapore, and Germany are strengthening their workforces using apprenticeship programs. The components of these countries' programs vary, as does the level of holistic integration and participants' eligibility. In some countries, participation in apprenticeship programs is twice that in the US. Table 8.1 shows how US apprenticeship programs compare with similar programs in other countries.

During recent interactions at global apprenticeship conferences, we engaged with multiple organizations and contributors to apprenticeships from eight countries. Some of the same challenges faced domestically and internationally included:

1. How to inform policy in apprenticeship programs?
2. Who is involved in the apprenticeship process?
3. Why has it been so difficult for apprenticeship programs to gain traction with employers?
4. What are some opportunities for improvement to existing programming?

Table 8.1 Comparison of Different Countries' Apprenticeship Programs

Country	*Programs*	*Funding*	*Benefits*
Spain	• Dual Vocational Education and Training (VET) program • Combines classroom and hands-on training	• Co-funded by the government, regional entities, and employers • Trainees receive a stipend	• High employability post-completion • Employers often hire apprentices after training • Access to skills certification
United Kingdom	• Apprenticeship programs from level 2 to level 7 (degree level) • Standards align with industry	• Funded through the Apprenticeships Levy for larger employers • Government co-funding for small employers	• Wage for apprentices, depending on age and year • Clear progression paths to degree-level and professional qualifications • Broad industry support
Singapore	• SkillsFuture Work-Study Program • Industry-centric training for sectors like tech and finance	• Government heavily subsidizes training costs • Employer co-funding	• Participants receive a salary • Pathways to diploma or degree programs • Skills alignment with high-demand sectors
Germany	• Dual Apprenticeship System with over 300 officially recognized professions • Close industry alignment	• Funding is split between the government and companies • Apprentices receive wages from employers	• Globally recognized, highly structured system • Wage and benefits for apprentices • Strong post-program employment rates
United States of America	• Registered Apprenticeship Program (RAP) with over 1,000 occupations • Industry-driven, state-supported	• Funded through federal and state grants, as well as employer contributions	• "Earn and learn" model with wages • Industry-recognized credentials • High-earning potential post-apprenticeship

SME Reflection: Challenges of Apprenticeship Programs

Nicholas D'Antonio, PhD, Project Engineering Manager, has worked in the aerospace and defense industry throughout his career. He has collaborated with organizations focused on talent acquisition and development, with a specialization in national and international apprenticeship programs.

Developing apprenticeships in technical fields like manufacturing and engineering faces challenges primarily due to the need to adapt existing employer practices to align with apprenticeship structures. In manufacturing, many employers already rely heavily on on-the-job training. They may not see the need for formalized classroom education, particularly in touch labor positions where specialized skills are often learned on the floor. Shifting this perspective to incorporate structured classroom learning can be difficult, as it may disrupt existing hiring and training methods. The challenge is even more pronounced for engineering roles, as a bachelor's degree is typically seen as a prerequisite for hiring rather than a component that can be pursued alongside on-the-job training. Employers must rework these established practices to accommodate an apprenticeship model that intentionally integrates both on-the-job and classroom learning (related technical instruction).

Apprenticeships should also include a progressive wage structure, which rewards apprentices with incremental pay increases as they advance and gain additional skills. This requires employers to adjust performance and compensation practices to meet apprenticeship standards, which can feel unfamiliar or impractical for those with established protocols. Addressing these challenges involves reworking hiring, training, and compensation systems to fully realize the benefits of an apprenticeship program. Many employers find the burden of these changes outweighs the benefits of establishing formal apprenticeship programs.

HR Action Step: Build Awareness for Apprenticeship Programs for Employers

There are multiple opportunities for employers to build an apprenticeship program through informal or formal means. The Department of Labor offers a formal Registered Apprenticeship Program serving multiple industries. Many employers are apprehensive about the programs' requirements. However, with clear guidance and support, employers will see that the benefits outweigh the preparation. Numerous resources are available to help navigate program implementation. We provide links to some of them below, including industry-specific and company-focused options.

Resources

Apprenticeship Assistance

- Federal Guidance: ApprenticeshipUSA,[10] a resource sponsored by the Department of Labor (DoL), promotes a "learn-while-you-earn" model, offering a one-stop source to connect career seekers, employers, and educational partners. Employers can find additional resources and fact sheets to design, develop, and implement programming. Guidance is provided on legislation, regulations, and policy.
- State-Wide Apprenticeship Data: To view current active apprenticeship data by state, access the "apprentices by state" interactive dashboard on apprenticeship.gov.[11]

Field-Specific Programs

- North America's Building Trades Unions (NABTU)[12] is an organization representing US and Canadian skilled construction workers, with an aim to increase union construction jobs and promote higher wages and better benefits. They partner with employers to train thousands of new workers through apprenticeships and skilled training programs.
- ToolingU-SME,[13] a nonprofit that offers over 600 online manufacturing courses, certifications, and resources for apprenticeship programs. Their pre-apprenticeship programs have preset curricula that can be customized or incorporated into existing curricula. The program meets the criteria to enter Registered Apprenticeship Programs (RAPs).

Company-Specific Apprenticeships

Larger firms have developed their own programs through the Department of Labor's Registered Apprenticeship Program. Small and medium-sized firms are also eligible to participate. We have worked with small businesses that have successfully initiated programs within manufacturing. However, the best resource for understanding more about apprenticeships is ApprenticeshipUSA.

- Large Business: Lockheed Martin,[14] which is proclaimed as a US Department of Labor Apprenticeship Ambassador through ApprenticeshipUSA, offers apprenticeships in aircraft maintenance, software engineering, and cybersecurity, employing 4,000 apprentices across 22 states.
- Medium-Sized Business: Kwest Group has developed a US Department of Labor-approved apprenticeship program focused on heavy civil

construction, with an emphasis on heavy equipment operation. The program combines virtual classroom instruction, hands-on field experience, and simulator training to support workforce development and employee retention and growth.

- Small Business Consortium: Northeast Ohio Manufacturing Apprenticeship Consortium (NOMAC), an apprenticeship consortium created by WIRE-Net (Westside Industrial Retention & Expansion Network) to accommodate administration, curriculum development, and state registration for small and medium-sized firms.[15]

> ***HR Action Step: Understand Apprentice Experiences***
>
> If you adopt an apprenticeship program, ensure that apprentices feel supported and prepared to enter the field. If there are barriers to participation, understand and address them to ensure apprentices' continued involvement in the industry after the program ends. There is limited research on why apprentices leave or choose not to pursue a career in the technical industry. Equally, more studies should address apprentices' support experiences with regard to race, gender, and special populations, such as veterans or those who are justice-involved.

Research Study

In a recent research, we surveyed over 6,000 apprentices, yielding a 10 percent response rate. The purpose of the study was to determine apprentices' perceptions of readiness to transition into work, including how their experiences influence their willingness to persist in their chosen industry. Additionally, we investigated how belonging related to their willingness to enter the field.

The results indicated:

- Apprentices were confident to highly confident in their job readiness (variables included: course preparedness for full-time job, course and OJT preparedness for full-time job, ability to transfer skills gained to full-time job, and ability to demonstrate job readiness to future employers).
- Apprentices' positive experiences influenced willingness to work in the field (variables: beneficial experience, intentions to work in the field).
- Apprentices reporting a strong sense of belonging were more inclined to pursue careers within the industry after training (sense of belonging correlated with a perceived readiness for employment and industry engagement).

TXF-Aligned Research Recommendations

The following research recommendations represent a comprehensive approach to advancing organizational equity and effectiveness through strategic human resources practices. Grounded in the TXF, these recommendations address critical gaps in compensation equity, hiring transparency, training accessibility, and career advancement systems. Each recommendation is designed to strengthen both HRD operations and strategic workforce development, creating a more inclusive and competitive organizational environment. By implementing these evidence-based interventions, organizations can simultaneously improve employee satisfaction, reduce disparities across demographic groups, and enhance long-term talent retention and development outcomes.

1. **Comprehensive Pay Equity Analysis and Compensation Structure Reform:** To improve pay equity and access, a thorough review of organizational compensation structures is recommended. This initiative involves conducting a detailed compensation audit across all job levels, departments, and demographic categories to identify systemic pay disparities. The research should examine base salaries, bonuses, equity compensation, and total rewards packages, comparing them against internal equity benchmarks and external market data. This approach directly aligns with the development of equitable HRD practices by establishing transparent, data-driven compensation frameworks that reduce arbitrary pay variations and ensure fair remuneration regardless of gender, race, or other protected characteristics. The implementation of standardized pay structures with clear advancement pathways will enhance organizational competitiveness in talent markets while promoting internal fairness and employee trust.
2. **Implementation of Strategic Transparency-Based Hiring Practices to Expand Talent Pipelines:** The implementation of strategic HR hiring practices to expand talent pipelines requires establishing transparent and consistent protocols across all stages of the recruitment and selection process. This recommendation involves developing standardized job descriptions with clear competency requirements, implementing structured interview protocols with validated assessment criteria, and creating transparent communication channels that keep candidates informed throughout the hiring process. Organizations should establish partnerships with diverse talent sources, including Historically Black Colleges and Universities (HBCUs), Hispanic-Serving Institutions (HSIs), community colleges, and professional organizations serving underrepresented groups. The research should evaluate the effectiveness of blind

résumé screening, diverse interview panels, and competency-based assessments in reducing implicit bias. This strategic HR practice aligns with organizational goals to build more diverse, qualified talent pipelines while ensuring consistency and fairness between employers and across hiring managers. By implementing evidence-based transparency measures, organizations can attract broader talent pools, improve candidate experience, reduce time-to-hire, and ultimately strengthen workforce diversity and quality.

3. **Universal Access to Professional Development and Training Programs to Close Demographic Gaps:** To reduce demographic gaps across leadership and technical roles, comprehensive changes to training and professional development systems are recommended to ensure universal access across the whole organization. The research should investigate current barriers to training participation, including scheduling conflicts, geographic limitations, financial constraints, and awareness gaps. Organizations should implement multiple modalities of training delivery, including on-demand digital learning, mentorship programs, cohort-based development initiatives, and sponsored external certification programs. Special attention should be given to creating leadership development pathways specifically designed to address the unique challenges faced by women and employees from underrepresented racial backgrounds. This initiative aligns with HRD practices by establishing equitable access mechanisms while also supporting strategic workforce planning through systematic skill development. The goal is to create a culture of continuous learning where all employees, regardless of their starting position, demographic background, or work location, have equal opportunities to acquire new competencies, advance their careers, and contribute at their highest potential.
4. **Transparent Career Advancement Systems to Ensure Equitable Promotion Pathways:** To ensure career advancement equity, the establishment of clear transparency regarding promotion processes represents a critical HRD practice. This recommendation involves developing and communicating explicit promotion criteria, timelines, and decision-making processes that eliminate ambiguity and reduce the potential for bias in advancement decisions. Organizations should implement regular talent review calibrations, establish clear performance metrics tied to promotion eligibility, and create visibility into career pathways through competency frameworks and role progression maps. The research should examine promotion rates across demographic groups, identify bottlenecks in advancement pipelines, and evaluate the effectiveness of sponsorship and advocacy programs in accelerating career growth for

underrepresented employees. Additionally, organizations should establish transparent appeals processes and regular promotion cycle communications to ensure all employees understand advancement opportunities and requirements. This systematic approach connects directly to HRD practices by standardizing promotion mechanisms while supporting strategic talent management through structured succession planning and internal mobility programs. By implementing transparent promotion systems, organizations can increase employee engagement, reduce turnover of high-potential talent, and build more diverse leadership pipelines that reflect the full spectrum of organizational talent.

These four research recommendations form an integrated framework for organizational transformation that addresses equity challenges while advancing strategic HR objectives. Collectively, they represent a shift from reactive, compliance-based approaches to proactive, strategic talent management that recognizes diversity, equity, and inclusion as fundamental drivers of organizational performance and innovation. The successful implementation of these recommendations requires sustained leadership commitment, cross-functional collaboration between HR and business units, investment in data infrastructure and analytics capabilities, and a willingness to make evidence-based adjustments to longstanding practices. Organizations that pursue this comprehensive approach will be better positioned to attract and retain top talent in increasingly competitive labor markets, build more resilient and adaptable workforces, and create organizational cultures where all employees can thrive and contribute to their fullest potential. The return on investment extends beyond traditional HR metrics to encompass enhanced innovation capacity, improved decision-making through cognitive diversity, stronger employer brand reputation, and sustainable competitive advantage in the marketplace.

In addition to our research, we have had the opportunity to learn from other subject matter experts who own businesses that primarily provide services to apprentices. The SME reflections provide context for how we can scale the talent pipeline, starting with engaging the youth population. The intentionality of this approach ensures new talent is introduced to careers in the technical space. Similarly, reflections from the UK organization, Apprentis, offer insights into the differences between US and other globally based programs.

SME Reflection

During the global session noted, we spoke with two UK entrepreneurs, from the company Apprentis, who shared their perspectives on how UK apprenticeship programs may differ from those in the US. The entrepreneurs are former apprentices who have established Apprentis to support youth in apprenticeships (18–24) across various industries.

We asked the following questions:

Question: How do you feel UK apprenticeship programs benefit apprentices as compared to US programs?

Response: The UK has wider recognition of apprenticeships across industries, including digital technology, finance, engineering, healthcare, and construction. Another key strength of the UK system is the way academic learning is tied directly to the workplace. Apprentices can immediately practice and implement what they learn, making the model more practical than theoretical. This constant cycle of "learn → practice → refine" creates a win-win: apprentices build confidence, and employers see fresh knowledge applied in real time. However, both countries face the same challenge: scaling apprenticeships as a mainstream choice, not an alternative or "lesser" option to university.

Question: In the UK, what best practices have employers implemented to ensure successful outcomes?

Response: Employers include dedicated mentoring and career coaching into apprenticeship programming. Employers who invest in apprenticeships as a pipeline for leadership and innovation tend to see the highest returns. By offering continuous development beyond the apprenticeship, [employers] are able to retain talent and support long-term careers.

Apprenticeships are the future of work and education, but to unlock their full potential, organizations must:

- actively challenge stigma by positioning apprenticeships as prestigious, future-ready pathways;
- build inclusive recruitment strategies that attract diverse candidates, especially in industries where representation is low;
- foster a culture of growth by providing clear progression opportunities post-apprenticeship;
- partner with platforms and organizations (like Apprentis) that champion lived experience and help bridge the gap between policy, education, and employer practice.

Apprenticeships, when done right, are not just about filling vacancies; they are about building resilient, diverse, and innovative workforces for the future.

Leadership Development Programs

Research suggests that the selection and handpicking of leaders on a predetermined track or program can introduce bias and favoritism into the advancement process. To combat this, we suggest the following tactic: develop a specific leadership track that clearly identifies promotion criteria, then communicate those criteria consistently and frequently. Create equal access and opportunities for all staff to advance through the ranks and offer support throughout the process.

HR Action Step: Develop Equitable Leadership Programs

1. **Leadership Buy-In Matters:** Leaders must endorse all training programs, especially leadership development. Following leadership programming, emerging leaders should be trusted with the responsibilities of their new role and given permission to make decisions on behalf of the organization without scrutiny or criticism.

Case Study Example: *A minority-owned business leader in manufacturing shared his experiences as an employee. He said as an employee he was often overlooked for new opportunities because he "didn't have the training" to meet the job requirements. Recognizing that this strategy was systematic and intentional, he vowed to do things differently if he ever ran his own company. Today, he offers complete autonomy and trust to his fellow leaders and staff throughout the organization.*

2. **Representation Matters:** Multiple backgrounds, including races, ethnicities, languages, genders, and religious affiliations, must be represented in leadership.

Case Study Example: *A small business manufacturer who hires immigrants who speak multiple languages ensures that his leadership staff has a representation of various ethnicities who speak those languages. Employees are motivated to seek advancement because they see that the leader prioritizes advancement for all staff.*

3. **Underrepresented Minority Leaders Need Ongoing Support:** Promoting leaders through a formalized leadership program is beneficial and affords them opportunities to grow in the field, but don't stop the support once they get the new title.

Case Study Example: *Especially with regard to women of color, known as the Glass Cliff, women are promoted during highly volatile organizational states without training or mentorship. Our research indicates that this approach places stress on women leaders and may cause them to exit the field prematurely.*

HR Action Step: Promote a Learning Culture

Based on the technical industry, the learning culture may change, evolve, and transform in different ways. For example, in construction, the learning culture may be driven by the leadership's ability to offer hands-on training opportunities, prioritize safety education, and promote continuous skill development on the job site.

1. **Learning Management System and Other Technologies:** Micro-credentials and digital badges are common in technical industries. They can be formally presented by larger associations through ToolingU-SME, which is a non-profit professional association (part of SME) that advances manufacturing, or developed internally (by company training coordinators) to reinforce learning.[16] While learning management systems can be costly to adopt, they provide live, consistent access to learning for all employees. While we focus on diverse demographics, this approach supports individuals who may not always speak up in group settings (introverts) and those who drive innovation from within by identifying opportunities and creating solutions (intrapreneurs), helping to surface their ideas and contributions.

Examples: *Moodle, Canvas, Brightspace, Blackboard.*

2. **Gamification:** The use of simulations, virtual reality (VR), and augmented reality (AR) expands professional development knowledge in technical industries in a safe, proximal location. All populations, whether rural, urban, or suburban, can participate. Equally, all people have an opportunity to learn new skills that may not otherwise be accessible. Gamification allows learning to occur on a larger scale across multiple platforms within various languages. The technology may allow for faster learning transfer, productivity, and comprehension for those who may be neurodiverse. Grants may exist to help small to medium-sized companies purchase and implement these upskilling options for staff.

Examples: *Simulation programs related to mission-critical operations within data centers, services to safety, or at-risk protocols in building automation.*

3. **Artificial Intelligence (AI):** How will AI be utilized in the organization? Specifically, are there certain pieces of equipment that will use AI as an embedded system? Or are there opportunities for leadership and HR practitioners to use AI as a mechanism to both offer new innovative training or elevate the traditional training methods?

SME Reflection

An SME offers the following insights for how AI can be used in manufacturing and other technical industries.

Question: How can AI contribute to training in manufacturing?

Response: AI can contribute to training in manufacturing in a number of ways. First, it can help with building personalized learning pathways. AI can be used to analyze a person's performance, learning style, and existing competencies, and use this information to create a personalized learning plan or customized training. I am also seeing several AI-powered VR/AR platforms offering immersive training experiences in trade occupations. AI can also provide simulations of hazardous situations to train employees on appropriate safety protocols, emergency responses, and OSHA requirements.

Question: What recommendations do you have for employers who are leery of adopting AI?

Response: Start small and start by looking at your key business processes. Look for small ways that AI can support current gaps in your key processes and try to get small, quick wins. Seek out other organizations that are further along and ask them about their AI journey. Talk with staff about their concerns about using and adopting AI.

Question: What types of products/trainings do you recommend/share with manufacturers as "types of products" that can be used with AI?

Response: AI-driven chatbots or virtual assistants that workers can consult during training or production to get instant answers on processes, standards, or troubleshooting. AI translation/chat tools for global teams, making training and instructions accessible across different languages. AI solutions that simulate machine failures and train workers on diagnosing and fixing potential breakdowns before they happen.

Question: Do you have any additional comments/recommendations for employers?

Response: Instead of trying to overhaul all training at once, employers should consider a phased approach. Start with a pilot program in a specific area or for a particular skill set. This allows for testing, gathering feedback, and refining the AI training solutions before a broader rollout. The manufacturing landscape is constantly evolving with new technologies and processes. Employers should use AI to foster a culture of continuous learning. AI can help identify emerging skill gaps and recommend relevant training modules.

HR Action Step: Performance Management Plan

Performance Management Plans provide employees with an opportunity to advance in a way that demonstrates clear, actionable, and transparent steps toward improvement and promotion. When leaders provide consistent feedback on performance and demonstrate equitable opportunities to expand knowledge, skills, and abilities, individuals feel more prepared and confident to accomplish their roles. To support improvement, we provide action steps to address organizational and individual development throughout the promotion process. Where applicable, real-world examples are provided.

1. **Develop Career Development Pathways/Plans:** Leaders and staff need to understand the pathways to development and promotion. When everyone understands what is expected of them for advancement and can recognize how to achieve their goals, the organization is more likely to succeed.
2. **Personalized Development Plans:** These are tailored training programs designed to meet each employee's specific career goals and developmental needs. Personalized learning paths demonstrate the company's investment in an employee's personal growth and career progression. In technical industries, process improvement approaches are widely studied to strengthen production through LEAN, which improves efficiency (speed and flow), and Six Sigma, which improves accuracy (quality and consistency). However, it is just as valuable to address the person's upskilling and knowledge gained. How is your organization mapping performance in an equitable way?
3. **Skills Matrix:** This is a formalized step-by-step promotion process to enable staff advancement. The Skills Matrix Tool contains prescriptive tasks to assess competencies or a set of production goals. Once specific milestones are met, staff can advance toward promotion. Skills matrices can be in paper-based format or digital

produced through software programs. While we do not have experience with all the tools, researching platforms to best fit your organization is recommended. There are industry-specific programs for manufacturing, engineering, and construction.

Case Study Example: *One manufacturing company uses this Skills Matrix model as an equitable training tool to both build professional development and ensure performance. Learning blocks are defined and aligned to job roles. Each role clearly maps to promotion points where accountability is maintained for both employee and supervisor. The career roles and salary ranges are clear and transparent to all staff.*

4. **Performance Management Systems:** Collect regular feedback from employees about the impacts of training transfer and opportunities for continuous improvement. Two performance systems should exist to address the upward mobility of staff promotion and retention systems (i.e., retention). Employee Performance Reviews should be equally balanced with Employee Stay Interviews to ensure retention of top talent. Companies should decide how evaluation criteria are tied to performance with clear and measurable objectives.

Informal Education

As part of the strategic planning, training should be embedded throughout the organization. All training opportunities should be equitable, accessible, and available. Informal programming can be initiated by leaders, staff, supervisors, or new hires. When the entire organization feels valued and their expertise and skills are appreciated, all staff will remain engaged and vested in their personal and organizational development.

HR Action Step: Collaborative Learning among Peers

As noted in our employees section of our TXF, the employee contributions not only influence retention, but they can adversely impact retention rates. Therefore, building a collaborative working environment, where peers can learn from and with one another, sets a strong foundation for growth and promotion across all divisions. Some examples are noted:

1. **Mentorship Programs:** While organizations can decide to offer a formal, structured program, the flexibility of informal programming within technical industries may prove more effective given time constraints and field limitations (e.g., access to work sites and compliance protocols). However, the benefits of mentor programs are

widely known to support and increase the professional development of mentors/mentees. To ensure equity, allow all staff the opportunity to participate in mentoring programs. Additionally, allow interpersonal input from staff on how mentorship engagements will be structured. If there can be a match/selection process, ensure all staff receive communications about the program. All leaders (from C-suite to supervisors) should participate to ensure full leadership buy-in. If mentors are external to the organization, provide the staff time for in-person or virtual meetings. There are many online platforms and toolkits that can assist with managing mentorship programs in-house or externally through other nonprofit organizations.

Case Study Example: *One manufacturing firm offers new hires a mentor-like, job-shadowing partner, called an "ambassador," to assist with general questions, acclimation to the organization, and knowledge-sharing in their new role. Leaders observed an increase in new-hire inclusion and confidence in doing their job from day one.*

2. **Self-Directed Learning:** This typically involves the use of audio-visual mediums such as books, podcasts, webinars, and workshops. As is common in small to medium-sized businesses, leaders may seek to learn about topics informally or individually with peers. Creating opportunities for all staff to learn informally is beneficial, motivating, and a morale booster. In highly technical organizations, staff spend time "taking action." By providing them with opportunities to engage with each other, teamwork and a sense of community and belonging are established. Additionally, time constraints in technical environments make it more difficult to participate in formal programs; this approach is meaningful and effective, promoting access, equity, and limitless growth opportunities.

Author Recommendation: *CEOs and leaders in the field can collectively assess their strengths and determine what topics they would like to expand upon. C-suite leaders who hold annual retreats should consider opportunities to transform the organization through learning alongside strategy.*

3. **Peer SMEs/Job Shadowing:** Empower employees to teach and transfer knowledge and expertise to other staff members. Each person brings unique skills and value to the organization. Providing a platform for peers to teach and cross-collaborate is inclusive and establishes trust, a sense of belonging, and loyalty—all attributes that foster belonging and improve retention.

Case Study Example: *One culturally and ethnically diverse firm hosts educational sessions for staff to teach peers about their customs and traditions (i.e., how holidays differ, etc.). Another company in the construction industry showcases top talent to teach subject matter to others in the organization. Topics can range from project management to hanging drywall.*

4. **Language Immersion:** Offer opportunities for non-English speakers to participate in English as a Second Language (ESL) classes or expand their knowledge of secondary languages used by staff and/or represented in your organization and community. For example, an employer might pay for access to language apps like Duolingo, Babbel, and Rosetta Stone.

Case Study Example: *One manufacturing firm partnered with a non-profit to come in and offer free English-language learning courses after their shift.*

Conclusion

HRD practices are essential mechanisms for employee retention in technical industries. By leveraging frameworks such as the Talent Expansion Framework (TXF), organizations can strategically address the multifaceted challenges of workforce development, from leadership training to staff-level upskilling. The HRD approach outlined in this chapter emphasizes that effective retention strategies require more than ad hoc training initiatives; they demand intentional, equitable programs that foster both technical skill advancement and career mobility. As demonstrated through the theoretical foundations and practical case studies presented, organizations that prioritize systematic training development, particularly those that embrace technology, ensure accessibility, and maintain competitive learning opportunities, position themselves to not only retain valuable talent but also build sustainable competitive advantages in rapidly evolving technical landscapes.

Notes

1 Shen, J., Chanda, A., D'Netto, B., and Monga, M. (2009). Managing Diversity Through Human Resource Management: An International Perspective and Conceptual Framework. *The International Journal of Human Resource Management*, *20*(2), 235–251.
2 Suber, L. R. (2023). Manufacturing Small Business Case Study: Successful HR Practices for Recruiting and Retaining Racially and Culturally Diverse Talent. [Doctoral dissertation, NC State University]. NCSU Libraries. https://catalog.lib.ncsu.edu/catalog/NCSU5800793
3 Boston Consulting Group (2023, December). The US Needs More Engineers. What's the Solution? https://www.bcg.com/publications/2023/addressing-the-engineering-talent-shortage
4 Associated Builders and Contractors (n.d.). Retrieved from https://www.abc.org/News-Media/News-Releases/abc-2024-construction-workforce-shortage-tops-half-a-million
5 National Association of Manufacturers (2021, May). 2.1 Million Manufacturing Jobs Could Go Unfilled by 2030. https://nam.org/2-1-million-manufacturing-jobs-could-go-unfilled-by-2030–13743/
6 Payan, T., Rodríguez-Sánchez, and Bonilla, M. (2024, October). Boost US Construction Workforce by Employing More Immigrant Labor. https://www.bakerinstitute.org/research/boost-us-construction-workforce-employing-more-immigrant-labor#_ednref23
7 U.S. Census (2022, October). More Women in Manufacturing Jobs in Every Age Group. https://www.census.gov/library/stories/2022/10/more-women-in-manufacturing-jobs.html
8 Bureau of Labor Statistics (2021). Labor Force Statistics from the Current Population Survey: Employed Persons by Detailed Industry, Sex, Race, and Hispanic or Latino Ethnicity. https://www.bls.gov/cps/cpsaat18.htm
9 Associated Builders and Contractors (n.d.). Retrieved from https://tinyurl.com/yve6jmbz
10 ApprenticeshipUSA (n.d.). Retrieved from https://www.apprenticeship.gov/employers/registered-apprenticeship-program
11 ApprenticeShipUSA (n.d.). Retrieved from https://www.apprenticeship.gov/data-and-statistics/apprentices-by-state-dashboard
12 North America's Building Trades Unions (n.d.). Construction Registered Apprenticeship. https://nabtu.org/apprenticeship-and-training/
13 ToolingU (n.d.). Manufacturing Apprenticeships. https://learn.toolingu.com/manufacturing-products-services/apprenticeships/
14 Lockheed Martin (n.d.). Apprenticeships. https://www.lockheedmartin.com/en-us/careers/candidates/students-early-careers/apprenticeships.html
15 SME (2017, July). Apprenticeship Programs Obtainable for Small Business Through Consortium Approach. Retrieved from https://www.sme.org/apprenticeship-programs-obtainable-small-business-consortium-approach
16 Tooling U (n.d.). Retrieved from https://learn.toolingu.com/about-us/our-story/

Chapter 9

Operational HR Practices: Considerations for Retention

The Role of Leadership in People-Centered Operations

We recognize that expanding talent pipelines is not something that happens by chance or simply because it aligns with organizational ideals. As leaders work to maintain business operations amidst talent shortages and growing skills gaps, their ability to adapt and respond effectively plays a significant role in supporting employee retention.

In the operational focus area of the framework (see Figure 9.1), operational practices must consider the employees' perspective to ensure they feel respected, valued, and appreciated in their work settings. Leaders should provide equal attention to the employee identity (who) and to how their sense of belonging within the organization is maximized. To guide organizational thinking on how to best center employee voice and which contributes to staff loyalty, connectedness, and longevity, we developed the operational section of the framework.

Leadership buy-in is critical for all HR practices. However, our research indicates that leaders do not simply drive the new culture, policy, and expectations for performance but their core values shape how they approach diversity and retention in their organizations. During multiple case studies, we explored how leaders articulate the values and motivations that guide their approach to people-centered HR practices. We asked senior leaders including CEOs, C-suite executives, and other decision-makers involved in shaping organizational policies to reflect on the personal "why" behind their commitment to building strong, stable, and supportive workplaces. Their responses helped us identify several themes that can be examined further to spark meaningful discussion among HR teams and leadership groups. Understanding what drives leaders' decisions, whether connected to personal experience, organizational mission, or a broader commitment to employee well-being, provides valuable insight into how policies are interpreted, implemented, or resisted. Gaining clarity on leadership

DOI: 10.4324/9781003515937-10

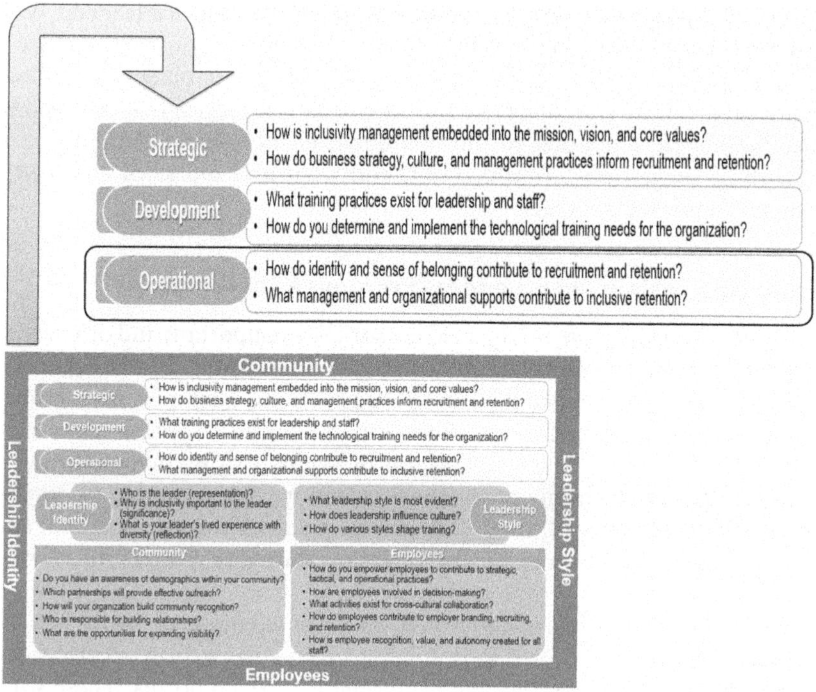

Figure 9.1 Operational Focus of Talent Expansion Framework. Image Credit: Laurel Royer (2026)

motivations can also highlight areas where additional professional development or organizational alignment may be needed.

Consider your own perspective, "Why is inclusivity important to you?" If the answer does not feel personal or you find yourself stuck in typical status quo answers, it might be time to dive deeper and understand why it is important. Your interest in this book already suggests that the topic holds meaning for you and exploring that meaning can help strengthen your leadership approach.

Leadership WHYs

We gave away the lead in the paragraph above, not sure if you caught it or not, but most leaders answered the question of WHY, for them, it remained a personal pursuit. Several shared sentiments such as, "This is the way I grew up," "We were raised to take care of the community," or, as one minority leader explained, "My lived experience shaped my perspective." Another added, "I always want to offer the culture and opportunities I didn't have."

This question really gets to the leadership identity of our leaders. Who are the leaders? This section of operational considerations will require a unique lens for each leader to understand. While our blueprint outlines action steps for diversifying talent pools, we do not suggest that our recommendations are a one-size-fits-all approach. Leaders stand at the helm of how these suggestions are rolled out, and what may work for one leader may not work for another.

Emerging Insight into Leader–Employee Interactions

A real-world example from the field illustrates an important and often overlooked dynamic in leadership and employee interactions. In one organization, a leader implemented a blind hiring process to ensure fairness, reduce bias, and highlight candidate skills and qualifications. After reviewing applications, the leader invited several individuals to participate in interviews. Although the hiring process was intentionally designed to be equitable and focused on merit, some candidates appeared hesitant, guarded, and visibly uncomfortable once the conversation shifted to a direct interaction with the leader.

Much of the existing research focuses on how employees from historically underrepresented or non-dominant groups navigate workplaces led by individuals who represent long-standing leadership norms. These studies often explore the challenges those employees encounter when adapting to organizational cultures shaped by traditional expectations. However, our findings indicate that the reverse dynamic also deserves careful attention. In settings where leaders bring backgrounds, identities, or experiences that differ from what employees commonly expect, candidates and staff may experience uncertainty or discomfort that is rarely acknowledged or examined.

For example, in one manufacturing case study, a minority company owner expressed hiring challenges when seeking to hire non-minority candidates. Despite offering competitive wages, title, and benefits, the candidates were not highly engaged during the interview process, "appearing uninterested" in the role. He questioned whether the candidates' discomfort reflected an unwillingness or bias toward reporting to a leader outside their own race. Although some research is emerging to examine subtle and overt behavior among ethnic minority leadership and its impact on leadership competence, more in-depth studies are needed to examine experiences during the hiring process.[1]

This discomfort is not simply an interpersonal issue. It signals a deeper and underexplored barrier that can affect communication, trust-building, performance conversations, and overall workplace cohesion. When candidates or employees hesitate to engage fully with leaders who do not align with their internalized expectations of who a leader should be, the result can undermine the effectiveness of individuals, teams, and the organization as a whole. This insight points to an important direction for future inquiry: Understanding why these reactions occur, how they appear in day-to-day interactions, and what organizational supports can reduce them is essential for strengthening workplace culture. Continued research in this area can help leaders anticipate challenges, foster more supportive team environments, and ensure that leadership intent is aligned with employee experience.

Bridging Leadership Insight to Operational Practice

As we reflect on how leaders shape workplace dynamics, it becomes clear that leadership influence must extend beyond hiring decisions and interpersonal interactions. Organizations routinely send leaders to retreats or planning sessions to establish budgets, set goals, and define strategic priorities. Yet one important question often remains unaddressed: Do these retreats include opportunities for leaders to develop deeper self-awareness and strengthen their understanding of how their actions, assumptions, and communication styles influence the workforce? Refer to Chapter 4 for leadership and Chapter 8 for training suggestions. In this chapter, we felt it was important to begin to craft how leaders are either the "spark" or "flame of change" or the "wind that snuffs out diversity," leading to problems with retention.

Business operations are significant, regardless of size, industry, or type (profit/nonprofit). However, our research indicates that organizational size and hierarchy may influence operational effectiveness. Our theoretical and practical expertise has been intentionally situated in small- to medium-sized manufacturing, construction, and engineering settings. However, large organizations will not only benefit from these recommendations but also have the financial prowess to amplify these cultural considerations.

Some reflection questions that influence operational practices include:

1. How do organizational size and hierarchy influence HR operations?
2. How does communication and transparency impact HR operations?
3. How does the firm demonstrate agility in changing technological times?
4. How does employee feedback contribute to organizational success?
5. How does your organization provide for cultural accommodations?

For each area of focus related to cultural considerations, we will provide recommendations on whether action steps may be interrupted, accelerated, or non-existent, based on the company's size, hierarchy, and organizational cultural aspects. Intentional operational practices for cultural consideration will be addressed throughout the chapter, with time and attention placed on both theoretical and practical data to support staff retention.

Business Size and Organizational Hierarchy

For this section, small businesses are defined as those with 0–150 employees, and medium-sized businesses are defined as those with 151–500 employees.

Practitioners and scholars agree that HR departments of one, those with sole responsibility for HR practices, often lack the capacity, knowledge, awareness, or access to resources, both financial and material, to ensure operational continuity. While this is typical of a small business, ad hoc approach to HR, it can occur with medium-sized businesses. In this instance, HR professionals are forced to seek out alternative third-party solutions through private consultants, nonprofit providers, or Professional Employer Organizations (PEOs).

Within technical industries, the ability to move swiftly is more critical as human interactions and engagement with automated tools directly impact productivity. If any part of the continuum is broken, as mentioned in the workplace chain of productivity, people may be overworked, leading to morale and retention issues.

Therefore, within a small business hierarchy, action steps must be accelerated to keep pace with the flexible actions required to ensure leaders and staff are prepared to manage complex issues that occur during the design (engineering), building (construction), and production (manufacturing) phases to meet customer needs. Specific practical communication and engagement processes for facilitating continuous discussion with staff are provided in the following sections. As one leader we interviewed mentioned, "we intentionally remove the invisible line among leaders and the factory floor," which facilitates an approachable, open dialogue across the organization. "Organizational hierarchy" leaders are viewed as immediately approachable and available to meet staff needs.

All Levels of Leadership

To counteract any issues with miscommunication of failed process implementation, all levels need to be present, engaged, and cognizant of staff happenings. For example, one of the case studies from the original dissertation research mentioned immigrant employees (husband and wife) who both worked for different parts of the manufacturing factory. Both employees were performing well at the organization. Still, issues with their benefits and eligibility forced them to choose between losing coverage or one of the employees would have to quit. Making more money, the husband stayed employed, and the wife left the organization. The managers, taking a personal interest in their staff's challenges, understood what hardships they were facing and stepped in to assist with finding suitable housing arrangements to help with financial issues. While this type of engagement may not have been possible in a medium- to large-sized plant, the ability to know their staff and engage was a strength and not only improved retention over time, but also increased recruitment through referrals.

Within small businesses, the flat hierarchy leads to more effective communication and engagement with staff. Building relationships among leaders and staff is essential to building rapport. Leaders do not want to be intrusive when seeking to understand staff. Still, they should be intentional about how they interact and learn how to assist in personally and professionally challenging times.

Communication

If organizations only think about traditional forms of communication, such as "how" we communicate, for example, email or phone, in this way we are missing the point. According to the *Oxford's Learner's Dictionary*, communication is "The act of transferring information from one place, person, or group to another." By this definition, all we mentioned above may work as strong factors of consideration. However, communication goes beyond the act of transferring information. The how, when, where, and to whom are considerations as well. If we are working toward building a diverse workforce, especially in technical settings, communication must go deeper.

First, we must make note of the types of communications. When the communication is *people-specific*, Engaging employees effectively requires leaders to understand and adapt to the diverse ways people communicate. Strong interpersonal, intercultural, and visual communication practices help ensure all staff feel heard, respected, and equipped to succeed. The following skills emphasize how leaders can foster inclusive, supportive interactions across roles, languages, and abilities.

Interpersonal Communication

Definition: The exchange of messages between individuals through speaking, writing, or shared systems of signs or behaviors.

Example: Healthy communication between leaders, supervisors, and staff should be continuous and open. Leaders must be willing to interact directly with front-line personnel, including field staff and factory floor workers, to reduce hierarchical barriers and demonstrate that every employee's concerns are valued.

> ***HR Action Step: Initiate Friendly, Informal Check-Ins***
>
> Establish a routine cadence of check-ins to support engagement and rapport. This may include daily greetings and well-being touchpoints; monthly reflective conversations where staff share how they feel they are performing and any concerns; quarterly supervisor-led performance check-ins; and ongoing informal interactions woven into daily work.

Intercultural Communication

Definition: The exchange of messages between individuals whose cultural backgrounds may influence how verbal and nonverbal signals are interpreted.

Example: Language differences may pose challenges for employees who speak English as a Second Language (ESL). Adjusting communication practices to enhance understanding is essential for employees' sense of belonging and their ability to perform job tasks. Leaders should also be aware of cultural norms—such as greetings, gestures, food practices, or religious observances—that shape interactions with staff and clients.

> ***HR Action Step: Provide Alternative Language Training:***
>
> A significant proportion of the workforce in technical industries (42% in construction and 34% in manufacturing) includes non-English speakers, with Spanish often being the primary additional language. Offering ESL support for employees and optional language learning (e.g., Spanish courses for English-speaking staff) strengthens communication and safety. This is particularly important in construction, manufacturing, engineering, and other technical settings where multilingual employees are common.

> ***HR Action Step: Increase Leadership Awareness of ESL Tools:***
>
> Research consistently shows that language barriers affect participation and advancement in many entry-level and technical roles. Employers can mitigate these challenges by leveraging technology tools that support language development and comprehension. Increasing leaders' awareness of practical ESL-support technologies can improve retention and operational efficiency. Tools with demonstrated effectiveness include:

1. goFLUENT[2]
2. EnGen[3]
3. ESL and literacy organizations

Visual and Digital Communication

Definition: The use of visual forms, such as graphics, signs, design elements, and digital imagery to convey information, often through electronic platforms.

Example: Visual communication strategies are especially valuable for employees who are hearing-impaired, neurodivergent, or who process information more effectively through images rather than spoken or written language.

> **_HR Action Step: Embrace Communication Technologies_**
>
> Incorporate visual tools such as video emails, short recorded updates, or Slack announcements with graphics or captions. Many non-English speakers and employees with disabilities rely heavily on mobile devices and digital tools, making visually accessible communication essential for reaching the entire workforce across varied work environments.

Engagement-Specific Communication Skills: Effective employee engagement relies on communication practices that go beyond day-to-day updates. Leaders must intentionally communicate in ways that build trust, reinforce clarity, and strengthen employees' connection to the organization. The following skills represent core communication behaviors that support meaningful engagement and help create an environment where employees feel informed, valued, and equipped to contribute.

Strategic Communication

Definition: The purposeful use of communication by an organization to fulfill its mission.

Example: Strategic communication builds trust and transparency. It requires clear, consistent messaging and ongoing opportunities for clarification and feedback.

> **_HR Action Step: Use Multiple Communication Channels + "Doubleback"_**
>
> A best practice emerging from our ongoing work is a strategy we call "doubleback." This refers to a leader's willingness to revisit important

information to ensure it was both received and understood. For instance, a leader might follow up a mass email with a brief text reminder or mention key points again in a team meeting to reinforce understanding.

Crisis Communication

Definition: The collection, processing, and dissemination of information needed to effectively respond to a crisis situation.
Example: Technical environments such as factories, field sites, or labs often require employees to understand specific emergency procedures. Feeling prepared and confident is essential for staff across all roles, backgrounds, and identities. Strong crisis communication ensures that all employees know how to respond during emergencies, from unexpected illness to active-shooter situations.

Educational Communication

Definition: The exchange of information and ideas in an educational setting, including teaching, learning, and academic interaction.

Example: Within technical industries, on-the-job training is a foundational and daily occurrence. The ability to communicate and or demonstrate a task is critical. All staff, regardless of cultural, ethnic, racial, or gender background, need to understand "how" to do their job. If supervisors lack training in communicating across demographics, retention will be a problem. See Chapter 4 for other tips.

Building Trust and Transparency

- How can employers use technologies and communication strategies to ensure trust across the organization? Trust is a factor.
- Does leadership feel comfortable listening to what the staff is saying?
- Are personal issues, such as work-life balance, religious holidays, and even deportation concerns something that can be broached with leadership?

More input and feedback from staff are needed to help employers navigate personal issues effectively and create opportunities for flexible schedules, childcare needs, and other barriers.

Conclusion

Operational HR practices centered on retention cannot succeed without committed and engaged leadership at all levels of the organization. Leaders serve as the critical link between strategic HR initiatives and their practical implementation within the framework's operational focus area. By actively supporting employee identity, fostering a culture of loyalty and connectedness, and demonstrating genuine investment in employee development, leaders transform retention strategies from policy documents into lived organizational realities. As the research indicates, leadership buy-in extends beyond mere approval; it requires leaders to embody and champion the people-centered values that sustain talent pipelines and create work environments where employees choose to stay and grow. Ultimately, the success of any retention-focused operational practice hinges on leadership's willingness to prioritize the employee perspective alongside organizational objectives, creating a mutually beneficial relationship that strengthens both individual careers and organizational capacity.

Authors' Tips for Strengthening Engagement and Retention

Beyond formal policies and procedures, small everyday practices can significantly influence how supported and connected employees feel. The following Authors' Tips offer practical, relationship-centered strategies that leaders can implement immediately to deepen trust, strengthen workplace culture, and enhance long-term retention.

Authors' Tip #1:

Create and maintain a resource guide for supervisors and staff that includes community providers, supportive services, and relevant external resources that employees may benefit from.

Authors' Tip #2:

Where appropriate, welcome family and friends into designated workplace engagement experiences or events, recognizing that external support systems often contribute to employee stability, motivation, and long-term retention.

Authors' Tip #3:

Offer voluntary opportunities for employees to share aspects of their cultural backgrounds or lived experiences in non-intrusive ways that support learning and connection across teams.

Building a stable and committed workforce requires attention to both operational practices and the human side of work. When leaders invest in creating clear systems, communicating consistently, and understanding the lived experiences of their employees, organizations are far better positioned to retain talent, reduce turnover, and strengthen performance over time. As you move forward, use these insights to inform practical action in your setting and continue refining what works best for your organization and the people who power it.

Notes

1 Anderson, A. J., Ahmad, A. S., King, E. B., and Gilrane, V. (2019). Subtle and Overt Behaviors Toward Ethnic Minority Leaders and the Moderating Role of Competence. *Journal of Leadership & Organizational Studies*, *26*(3), 372–388. doi:10.1177/1548051819859289

2 goFLUENT (n.d.). Retrieved from : https://www.gofluent.com/us-en/

3 EnGen (n.d.). Retrieved from: https://getengen.com/

Chapter 10

Employee Voices Amplify Retention

Employee retention is a significant challenge for organizations in today's competitive job market. High turnover rates not only affect productivity but also increase costs associated with recruitment, training, and the loss of institutional knowledge. A critical yet often underutilized tool in addressing retention issues is employee feedback. By actively listening and responding to employee voices, organizations can significantly enhance job satisfaction and reduce turnover. This chapter explores the role of employee feedback in shaping retention strategies, offering practical methods for gathering and incorporating this input into human resource (HR) practices.

The Importance of Employee Feedback in Retention

Employee feedback is invaluable in understanding the factors that contribute to both job satisfaction and dissatisfaction. When employees feel that their concerns, suggestions, and opinions are heard, they are more likely to develop a sense of belonging and commitment to the organization. This connection directly influences retention rates, as employees who are satisfied with their work environment are less likely to seek opportunities elsewhere. Many successful organizations have recognized the importance of employee voices in shaping their retention strategies. By fostering a culture of openness and responsiveness, these organizations have seen improved retention, morale, and overall productivity.

Talent Expansion Framework (TXF)—Employees Focus

As we mentioned in the introduction to the Talent Expansion Framework (TXF), all contributors from employers, the community, and employees can take responsibility for supporting attraction, recruitment, and retention. As an organization, it is necessary to understand the influence your employees have on the organizational culture, both in building it and maintaining it.

DOI: 10.4324/9781003515937-11

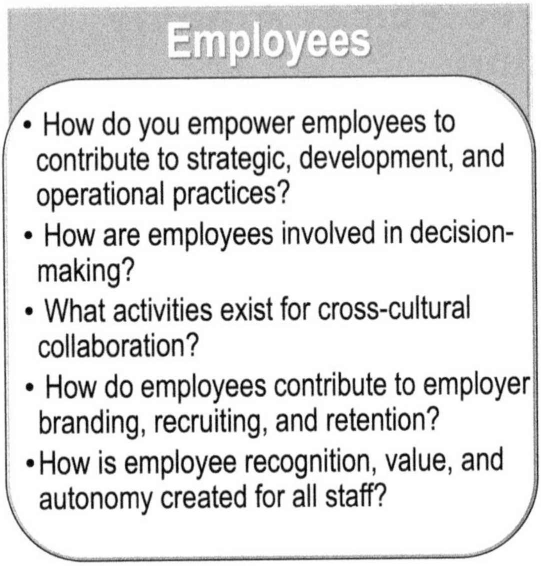

Figure 10.1 Employee Focus of Talent Expansion Framework. Image Credit: Laurel Royer (2026)

The TXF's focus on employees provides organizational questions to help guide inclusive recruitment. By evaluating *"what"* employees have input on within the HR practices, organizations can ensure they are effectively incorporating their knowledge, experience, and feedback. Similarly, asking *"how"* they engage with HR practices allows leaders to gauge their level of satisfaction within the organization. Five employee focus questions guide employees' action-oriented approach (see Figure 10.1).

Organization-Wide Engagement

Question 1, "*How do you empower employees to contribute to the strategic, development, and operational practices?*", allows employers to analyze how actively employees contribute to the three HR practice areas. For example, employees may contribute to the organization's mission, vision, or core values.

> **Strategic Example:** One company we spoke with consistently provides updates and training on the mission, vision, and core values. During this time, all staff have an opportunity to reflect, add, or recommend changes to the documents.

Development Example: Employees have the opportunity to request training topics or workshops, or the flexibility to attend "trainings of their choice" within budgetary constraints.
Operational Example: Develop an employee engagement team to enable staff to bring concerns to the leadership team. Additionally, the employee engagement team member is permitted to participate in core team leadership meetings to represent employees' voices.

Question 2, "*How are employees involved in decision-making?*", allows employers to analyze the extent to which employees contribute to the decision-making process. For example, if they make no contributions, is it because they lack the authority to participate, or are they not interested or engaged with the organization? If they are disengaged, this may signal dissatisfaction and potential turnover.

Case Study Example: *An organization requested an update to its core values during annual meetings, yet no significant changes were implemented. Therefore, employees stopped contributing, with the belief that their opinions were not valuable.*

Peer-to-Peer Engagement

Question 3, "*What activities exist for cross-cultural collaboration?*" A sense of belonging contributes greatly to retention; when employees have the opportunity to collaborate across teams and cultures, creativity and innovation are sparked.

Community Engagement

Question 4, "*How do employees contribute to employer branding, recruiting, and retention?*" As formal representatives of your organization, your current and past employees "tell the story of life" at your organization. At a time when workers are seeking to develop work-life balance post-COVID, how you deliver on your employer reputation matters. For example, are staff dissatisfied and posting on social media? Or are they satisfied and referring friends and family to join your team?

Organizational Visibility

Question 5, "*How is employee recognition, value, and autonomy created for all staff?*" Building a culture where employees feel genuinely recognized and valued requires thoughtful and intentional effort. When individuals understand that their work is noticed and appreciated, they are more likely to feel connected to the organization and confident in their role within it. This sense of visibility helps cultivate trust, strengthen morale, and reinforces the belief that every person contributes meaningfully to the mission and daily functioning of the workplace. Recognition also communicates that leadership respects employees as people, not simply as positions or tasks to be completed.

Effective recognition can take many forms, and it does not necessarily require elaborate programs to make an impact. Simple practices such as supervisor or peer nominations for service-related contributions create opportunities to highlight moments when staff members go above and beyond. Pairing these acknowledgments with small rewards, such as an extra hour of leave, an early-release afternoon, or even a lighthearted "miss a meeting" pass, can provide a sense of appreciation while also adding a bit of fun to the work environment. These kinds of gestures are easy to implement and demonstrate that the organization pays attention to everyday efforts.

More formal or larger-scale recognition efforts can also play an important role. Some organizations hold annual appreciation events, offer modest gifts, or provide access to wellness programs or membership packages as a way to acknowledge the dedication of their staff. Others take a more ambitious approach, offering paid trips, special celebrations, or milestone recognitions that honor employees' long-term commitment. Regardless of the approach, the goal is to ensure staff members feel valued, supported, and connected to a workplace that takes pride in celebrating its people.

Ultimately, the most important aspect of recognition is the consistency and authenticity behind it. When appreciation becomes part of the organizational culture rather than an occasional initiative, employees are more likely to experience a sense of belonging and autonomy. A workplace that prioritizes visibility in this way not only strengthens engagement but also fosters an environment where individuals feel empowered to contribute their best work.

Methods for Gathering Employee Feedback

There are several effective methods organizations can use to gather employee feedback, each with its own strengths and limitations. Surveys and questionnaires are among the most common tools, providing a broad view of employee sentiment across different departments and levels. However, these methods can sometimes lack depth and fail to capture nuanced concerns. One-on-one interviews, especially during onboarding, change initiatives, and exit processes, offer more detailed feedback and can identify specific issues that may be impacting employee retention. Focus groups and open forums encourage group discussions, fostering a sense of community while gathering collective insights. While focus groups can encourage richer discussion where one participant's comment may spark memories or insights in others that might not surface in individual interviews, they also carry risks. Group settings can foster groupthink or allow dominant voices to overshadow differing perspectives. Therefore, it is essential to be mindful of power dynamics and potential imbalances when inviting participants to the focus group table. Additionally, anonymous feedback systems, such as suggestion boxes or digital tools, can help employees feel secure in sharing their concerns without fear of retribution.

Incorporating Employee Feedback into HR Practices

Collecting employee feedback is only the first step; the real impact comes from how organizations respond to that feedback. HR departments play a crucial role in processing and responding to employee feedback. One effective approach is to analyze feedback data to identify recurring themes and areas that require immediate attention. From there, HR can develop actionable insights to address specific concerns. Transparency is key in this process. Employees need to see that their feedback is not only heard but also acted upon. This can be achieved through regular updates, town hall meetings, or internal communications that highlight the changes made in response to employee input. Several organizations have successfully integrated feedback into their HR practices, resulting in significant improvements in employee retention and workplace satisfaction.

Foster a Culture of Open Communication and Trust

Leaders should prioritize creating an environment where employees feel safe to share honest feedback without fear of retaliation. Establish confidential channels for providing feedback and assure employees that their input will be respected and taken seriously. Transparency and openness will help build trust, making employees more likely to engage and participate in feedback initiatives. *If you want your employees to open up, ensure they understand that you're genuinely seeking their thoughts, not just seeking compliments.*

The Impact of Employee Feedback on Job Satisfaction

When organizations actively address employee concerns, it leads to higher levels of engagement and morale. Employees who feel that their feedback is valued are more likely to feel appreciated and invested in the organization's success. This, in turn, positively affects retention, as satisfied employees are less likely to leave their jobs. Moreover, employee feedback can lead to tangible improvements in work conditions, benefits, and career development opportunities, all of which contribute to long-term job satisfaction. Case studies of feedback-driven initiatives show that organizations can achieve measurable reductions in turnover by simply listening to and addressing the needs of their workforce. One example of best practices is deploying pulse surveys consistently (quarterly or biannually) to gather real-time feedback and promote continuous improvement. Pulse surveys can be as short as one question and address employee engagement, collaboration, cross-functional teams, or feelings of belonging. When pulse surveys are not deployed without action, it can decrease employee morale and performance.

Challenges in Utilizing Employee Feedback

Despite the clear benefits of incorporating employee feedback into retention strategies, organizations face several significant challenges in effectively utilizing this input. One of the most common barriers is the reluctance of employees to provide honest feedback due to fear of negative consequences. Employees may worry that speaking out will lead to retribution, such as reduced opportunities for promotion, negative performance reviews, or strained relationships with management. This fear can prevent employees from sharing their true feelings about workplace conditions, policies, or leadership practices, which ultimately limits the effectiveness of feedback initiatives. To overcome this, organizations must focus on building a culture of trust, where employees feel confident that their feedback will not be used against them. This involves creating safe and confidential channels for providing feedback, ensuring that the feedback process is transparent and unbiased. It also requires leaders to foster open communication and demonstrate a commitment to listening without judgment. After all, if your employees are afraid to speak up, it's like asking someone how they feel about your cooking . . . while you're still holding the knife.

Another challenge organizations face is skepticism. Employees may be hesitant to participate in feedback initiatives if they believe that their input will not lead to meaningful changes. This is particularly true if there has been a history of ignored feedback or if past promises for change have gone unfulfilled. Employees who feel that their voices have previously been disregarded may become disengaged and lose faith in the feedback process, viewing it as nothing more than a symbolic gesture. To address this challenge, organizations must not only solicit feedback but also follow through by demonstrating that they are taking concrete actions based on the feedback they receive. This requires timely and visible responses, such as implementing suggested improvements or communicating progress on the changes being made. Closing the feedback loop, where employees are informed about how their input is being utilized, can help rebuild trust and demonstrate that the organization is serious about addressing employee concerns.

Additionally, leadership buy-in is essential for creating a feedback-driven culture. Without the active support and participation of senior leaders, efforts to amplify employee voices are likely to falter. Leaders set the tone for the organizational culture, and their commitment to valuing feedback sends a powerful message to employees. If leaders view feedback as unimportant or a threat to their authority, employees are unlikely to feel comfortable sharing their thoughts and are less likely to believe that feedback will lead to change. To encourage leadership buy-in, organizations should emphasize the strategic value of employee feedback in improving retention, enhancing job satisfaction, and driving overall organizational success. When leaders recognize the direct link between feedback and positive outcomes, they are more likely to champion feedback initiatives and encourage managers at all levels to do the same. Because if you can't get the boss on board, it's like trying to steer a ship while the captain's still busy arguing with the map.

There are also logistical and structural challenges in collecting and effectively utilizing employee feedback. In large organizations, gathering feedback from diverse groups of employees with varying roles, responsibilities, and perspectives can be a complex task. Ensuring that feedback is representative of the entire workforce and not skewed by the voices of a few can be difficult. Moreover, analyzing and acting on large volumes of feedback can be resource-intensive, requiring dedicated time and personnel. Organizations must invest in systems and tools to streamline the feedback process, ensuring that feedback is not only collected efficiently but also reviewed and acted upon in a timely manner. Finally, organizations must be mindful of potential feedback fatigue. When employees are asked to provide input too frequently or in ways that feel burdensome, they may experience fatigue and disengage from the process. Feedback initiatives must strike a balance, ensuring that employees are given sufficient opportunities to share their voices without being overwhelmed by constant requests for input. Structuring feedback collection in a way that feels purposeful and not excessive can help maintain employee engagement.

Long-Term Retention Benefits from Amplifying Employee Voices

Organizations that consistently use employee feedback to drive improvements see long-term retention benefits. By creating a culture of continuous improvement based on employee input, they build loyalty and trust within the workforce. Over time, this leads to higher employee engagement, increased productivity, and a stronger organizational culture. Amplifying employee voices also helps organizations remain agile and responsive to changing needs, which is especially important in today's fast-paced business environment. The long-term effects of these practices are evident in lower turnover rates, better employee satisfaction, and a more positive overall organizational performance.

Author's Tip #1

Implement Diverse Feedback Methods: Don't rely on a one-size-fits-all approach. Utilize a combination of feedback collection methods, including surveys, one-on-one interviews, focus groups, and anonymous systems, to ensure that all employee voices are heard. This diversity enables leaders to capture both the broad sentiments of the workforce and the more nuanced concerns of individuals. Tailor your approach based on the feedback needs of different departments or teams. *Because sometimes, employees want to talk—and sometimes, they just want to check a box anonymously!*

Author's Tip #2

Act on Feedback Quickly and Transparently: Gathering feedback is just the first step. The key is in the follow-up. Leaders need to ensure that feedback is not only reviewed but also acted upon in a timely manner. Communicate with employees about the actions being taken as a result of their input. Share updates through meetings, emails, or town halls so employees know their voices are making a difference. *After all, feedback that vanishes into a black hole is about as useful as a suggestion box with no bottom!*

Author's Tip #3

Encourage Leadership Buy-In and Accountability: For feedback-driven retention strategies to be effective, leaders at all levels must buy into the importance of employee voices. Senior leadership should set the example, actively participating in feedback initiatives and demonstrating accountability for the changes being made. Emphasize the positive impact of employee feedback on retention and organizational success to motivate leadership engagement. *If your team sees the boss on board, they'll be more likely to believe the ship is heading in the right direction, and without any mutiny!*

Author's Tip #4

Balance Feedback Collection to Avoid Fatigue: While it's essential to gather regular feedback, overdoing it can lead to fatigue and disengagement. Make sure feedback initiatives are structured in a way that employees don't feel overwhelmed. Space out surveys and ensure that each feedback round serves a clear purpose, with tangible outcomes shared afterward. This keeps employees engaged and willing to participate. *Remember, feedback is like dessert: It's great in moderation, but if you keep serving it, people might just skip out!*

Conclusion

Employee feedback is a powerful yet frequently underleveraged tool for improving retention and strengthening organizational culture. When organizations move beyond viewing feedback as a one-time data collection exercise and instead treat it as an ongoing dialogue, employee voices become a critical driver of engagement, trust, and commitment. Listening to employees and acting on what is heard signals respect, transparency, and shared responsibility for organizational success. As demonstrated throughout this chapter, effective retention strategies are not built solely through compensation adjustments or policy changes but through intentional systems that invite, value, and respond to employee perspectives. Organizations that center employee voice are better equipped to identify emerging challenges, adapt to changing workforce expectations, and design solutions that reflect the lived experiences of their employees. In doing so, they foster a workplace environment where individuals feel heard, valued, and invested in the organization's future. Looking ahead, the future of retention depends on an organization's ability to continuously learn from its workforce and translate feedback into meaningful action. This ongoing process of listening, responding, and improving creates stronger retention outcomes and more resilient, innovative, and inclusive workplaces. Amplifying employee voices is not simply a strategy for reducing turnover but a pathway to building a thriving and sustainable organization.

Chapter 11

Reflections and Recommendations for Talent Expansion

In its current state, workplace policy related to people management has experienced rapid shifts, slowed momentum, and increased scrutiny. Many organizations, job seekers, and policymakers have chosen to step back from the high-visibility debates that once surrounded these efforts. Instead of focusing on the political landscape, this chapter emphasizes how our overarching framework can serve as a Talent Expansion Framework, enabling HR professionals to strengthen labor supply, stabilize pipelines, and support operational excellence in technical industries and beyond. As scholar-practitioners, we focus on practical, evidence-based strategies that help businesses invest in talent, meet production goals, and maintain competitiveness in key sectors such as manufacturing, construction, engineering, and other technical fields.

Although industry pressures have evolved, the United States continues to work toward advancing domestic production capacity, reshoring supply chains, and expanding critical infrastructure. New federal and state initiatives have fueled growth in sectors such as clean energy, offshore wind, advanced manufacturing, drone technologies, and housing innovation. Despite these investments, technical industries still face workforce shortages, underemployment, and uneven job quality across regions. To address these challenges, organizations must examine their HR systems (strategic, operational, and development) through the lens of who is responsible for implementing workforce practices and how those decisions shape talent pipelines. The focus now turns to realistic recommendations for policy awareness and practical action, grounded in the day-to-day realities of employers, educators, practitioners, and workers who sustain the vitality of the labor market. The outer edge of the Talent Expansion Framework (TXF) introduced in Figure 11.1 emphasizes the connectivity and influences that community, leadership, and employees have in implementing inclusive work practices. Building from that foundation, the following section summarizes key ideas from earlier chapters and aligns them with concrete steps for shaping organizational policy and practice.

DOI: 10.4324/9781003515937-12

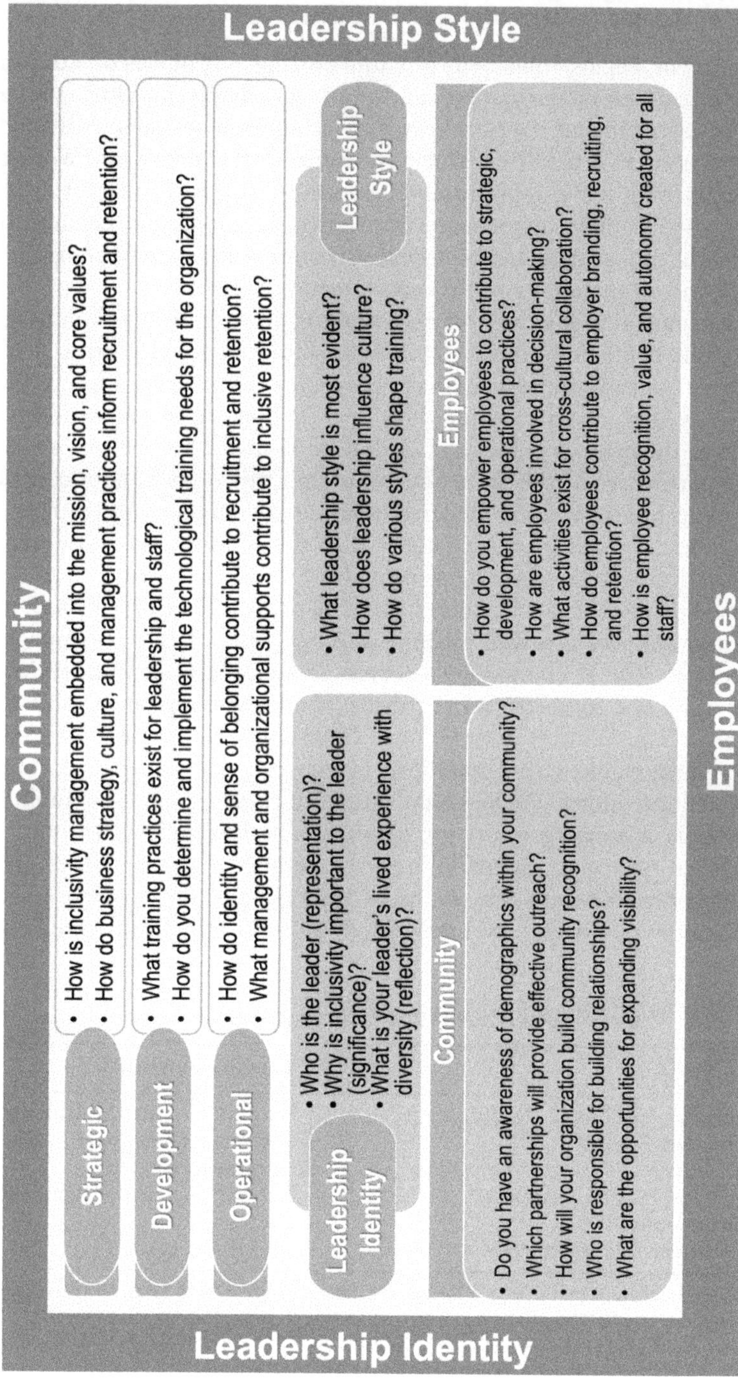

Figure 11.1 Talent Expansion Framework (TXF). Image Credit: Laurel A. Royer (2026)

Who Is Responsible for Recruitment?

Recruitment begins long before a job posting is published. Education, workforce development systems, and employer partnerships form the backbone of early pipeline development. Education provides early skill building and exposure that prepare learners for future career pathways. Workforce development systems align training, resources, and labor market needs to create a steady flow of prepared candidates. Employer partnerships offer real-world engagement and clear pathways into jobs, strengthening the relevance and sustainability of the recruitment pipeline.

Yet technical industries continue to struggle with visibility, messaging, and public perception, especially among younger and mid-career workers who may not fully understand the opportunities these fields offer. Technical industries often operate behind the scenes, making their contributions less visible to the general public and leading to limited awareness of available career pathways. At the same time, outdated stereotypes and inconsistent messaging hinder broader understanding, especially among younger and mid-career workers who may not realize the stability, growth potential, and upward mobility these fields provide.

As labor markets shift and industry roles evolve, both policy and practice must support renewed pipeline development. Chapter 6 emphasized the critical role of community partners in cascading recruitment, as the community is a cornerstone of attracting and recruiting talent. Numerous organizations, industry associations, think-tanks, nonprofits, and philanthropic groups have also developed frameworks to strengthen attraction and retention efforts. We highlight several of these resources in Table 11.1 to provide a starting point for employers seeking research, tools, and workforce strategies aligned with their operational needs. Where groups maintain broader missions, the focus here remains on workforce access, employment pathways, and talent development, not political agendas.

Table 11.1 Workforce-Related Action Groups

Action Group	*Framework Used*
Association for Talent Development	Talent Competency Framework
Jobs for the Future[a]	The Impact Employer Talent Framework[b]
Society for Human Resource Management	Talent Principles within SHRM
US Chamber of Commerce	US TIP Program

a Jobs for the Future (n.d.). Impact Employers: Putting People First. https://impactemployer.jff.org/impact-employer-model/

b Ward, C., Roberts, L., O'Connor, C. (2022). Jobs for the Future. *Preparing your company for the future of work by putting talent first.*

Policy Considerations for Recruitment

HR recruitment practices are shaped by professional standards, industry certifications, and regulatory guidance. Key associations such as the Society for Human Resource Management (SHRM), Human Resources Certification Institute (HRCI), and Association for Talent Development (ATD) influence HR competencies nationwide. Additionally, agencies such as the Equal Employment Opportunity Commission (EEOC) and the Office of Federal Contract Compliance Programs (OFCCP) provide compliance expectations that remain essential for organizations of all sizes. Staying current with employment law is not optional; it is a basic operational requirement. We recommend ongoing training, webinars, and federal updates to ensure that recruitment activities align with legal expectations and minimize organizational risk.

HR Practice

Moving from Theory to Practice

Recruitment sits at the intersection of strategy, culture, and operations. Leaders at every level, from executives to front-line supervisors, shape how organizations attract and retain workers. The TXF emphasizes both leadership identity (who leaders are) and leadership style (how they lead) as essential influences on workforce outcomes.

Leadership Identity

Understanding leadership identity is core to effective talent practices (see Figure 11.2). Northouse notes that leaders initiate and sustain relational connections within organizations, influencing communication, decision-making, and employee engagement.[1] Using Komives and colleagues' developmental categories,[2] employers can assess how leaders' experiences shape their approach to workforce issues. Table 11.2 contains guiding questions for reflection that keep the focus on talent management rather than ideological motivations.

Leadership Style

Eight widely recognized leadership styles remain relevant for technical sectors:

1. **Transformational Leadership:** Inspires innovation, continuous improvement, and forward-thinking approaches essential in rapidly evolving technical fields.

Table 11.2 Leadership Identity Reflection Questions

Leadership Identity Domain	*Reflection Questions*
Developing Influences	How do the leader's characteristics influence what talent is recruited in the future?
Developing Self	How does the leader's reflexivity impact their ability to lead?
Group Influences	How does the leader's identity influence who contributes to their talent management approach?
Changing View of Self and Others	Which lived experiences have shifted your perceptions of your purpose as a leader and those you lead?
Broadening View of Leadership	What aspects of leadership are challenging in practice?

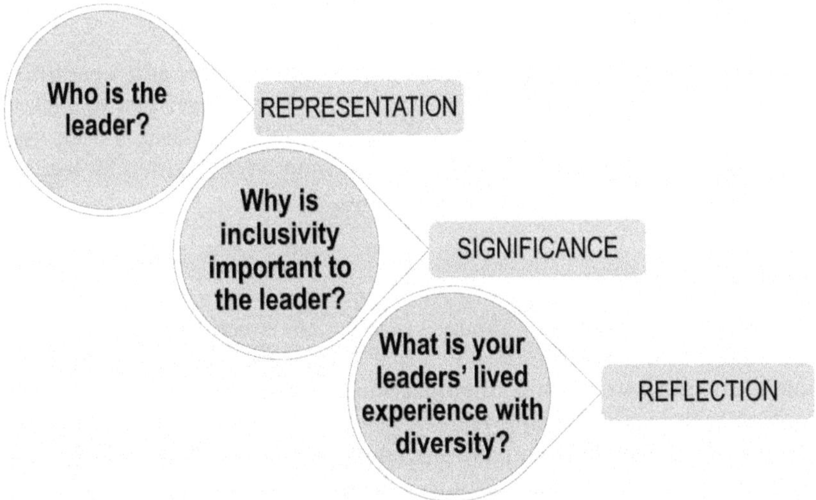

Figure 11.2 Leadership Identity Framework Questions. Image Credit: Laurel A. Royer (2026)

2. **Transactional Leadership:** Provides clarity, structure, and performance accountability suited for compliance-driven, safety-sensitive environments.
3. **Participative Leadership:** Leverages team expertise and shared decision-making, valuable where front-line workers hold deep technical knowledge.
4. **Servant Leadership:** Prioritizes employee development and well-being, which improves retention and builds a supportive learning culture in technical teams.

5. **Situational Leadership:** Adapts leadership style based on worker skill level, project phase, and operational context—critical in dynamic, project-based industries.
6. **Inclusive Leadership:** Ensures all voices are valued, increasing creativity, problem-solving, and team cohesion in diverse technical environments.
7. **Relational Leadership:** Builds trust, collaboration, and strong interpersonal connections, enhancing teamwork and knowledge-sharing in complex technical systems.
8. **Coaching Leadership:** Focuses on developing individual skills and competencies, vital for growing talent pipelines and upskilling workers in high-demand sectors.

Research consistently shows that leadership style influences workplace climate, employee retention, and culture. Technical fields frequently rely on transformational, transactional, and democratic leadership because these styles support clarity, structure, and project coordination. More recently, inclusive and relational leadership models have gained attention for their emphasis on communication, team cohesion, and shared problem-solving, qualities that directly strengthen safety, efficiency, and cross-disciplinary collaboration. The goal is not to promote a specific ideology but to equip leaders with approaches that improve performance, stability, and workforce continuity.

Our framework provides a broad range of questions that should be addressed across all leadership roles. When identifying who should be part of this discussion, include anyone who has authority, decision-making capacity, and employee oversight (including front-line leaders, superintendents, trainers), as well as all staff who lead people or projects.

Leadership Style Reflection Questions

Leadership style plays a central role in shaping how technical organizations operate, communicate, and develop their people. The following questions encourage reflection on how different leadership approaches influence workplace culture, guide expectations, and shape the design and delivery of training and talent development practices.

Reflecting on Leadership Style Awareness

- When you think about your daily decision-making, what traits or behaviors surface most naturally for you? What about when you are under stress or navigating uncertainty?
- How have past leaders or leaders around you, positive or negative, shaped the leadership tendencies you or your colleagues exhibit today?
- If someone else described your leadership style, what do you think they would highlight? Why?

Reflecting on Leadership's Influence on Culture

- How do leaders' actions, both intentional and unintentional, shape or contradict the culture your organization claims to uphold?
- In what ways does the alignment or misalignment between what leaders say and what they do influence trust, morale, and everyday workplace behavior?
- What aspects of your organization's culture can you directly connect to leadership decisions, responses to challenges, and communication styles?

Reflecting on Leadership's Influence on Training

- How do the things leaders value show up in the kinds of training they push, promote, or require?
- How have you seen leaders either help or get in the way of ongoing learning and development for staff?
- When has a leader's involvement made training better—and when has it made it harder or less effective?

The Community as a Workforce Partner

Local communities play a pivotal role in talent attraction and retention. Community colleges, workforce boards, regional partnerships, and civic organizations serve as connectors between employers and prospective workers. For technical industries, participating in community spaces enhances visibility, builds trust, and supports long-term pipeline development.

Organizations should consider several community-centered factors when developing their recruitment and workforce strategies. These include understanding demographic trends and labor market data, identifying partnership opportunities with regional education and workforce entities, strengthening brand recognition and organizational reputation within the community, and implementing intentional outreach strategies that increase visibility and connection with potential talent pools. Just as important is determining who within the organization will own community engagement responsibilities to ensure consistent, coordinated, and effective relationship-building efforts. These activities focus on employer visibility, career awareness, and alignment with regional labor needs, areas that remain firmly within workforce development and economic competitiveness.

Community-Based Questions

Building strong community connections is essential for sustaining a healthy talent pipeline and ensuring that programs remain relevant to local needs.

These questions encourage practitioners to examine how well they understand the communities they serve, how strategically they engage partners, and how effectively they position their organization within the broader local landscape. By reflecting on these areas, leaders can identify opportunities to strengthen visibility, expand outreach, and build meaningful relationships that support long-term workforce and organizational goals. The guiding questions from the community quadrant are noted below. For additional context and reflection, see Figure 11.1. These questions provide context for understanding the external community (talent pool) and the supporting workforce ecosystem (partners).

- Do you understand the population trends and priorities within the community?
- Which partnerships will provide effective outreach?
- How will your organization build community recognition?
- Who is responsible for building relationships?
- What are opportunities for expanding visibility?

Community is not only a place but a group of individuals with like-minded attributes, values, and goals. Understanding the community is just as important as understanding your customer. Your community is the backbone to success. To expand locally, regionally, or statewide, your neighbors to the left and right can offer "intros" to the talent in your area. As previously mentioned, most communities have workforce boards, community colleges, and other informal networks. Seek out opportunities to get to know your populations, partners, and competition by intentionally engaging in their environments and observing how they operate. For populations, this might include visiting training sites or campuses, holding listening sessions with learners or workers, and reviewing enrollment or performance data to understand their needs and motivations. With partners, you can deepen knowledge by attending advisory council meetings, conducting site visits, or checking in regularly with industry supervisors about evolving skill demands. Understanding competition involves analyzing their program offerings, attending their public information sessions, reviewing marketing materials, or observing recruitment events to see how they position themselves. Together, these activities build a clearer picture of the broader landscape and strengthen strategic planning. The more you know about the area, the better equipped you are to fully operationalize your recruitment and retention strategies.

HR Action Step: Designate a Community Engagement Liaison

Most importantly, in this community section, determine who will be tasked with this new aspect of their job description, including the possibility of hiring a new staff member. While most small and medium-sized businesses lack the time, money, or resources to handle this role, delegating it can yield significant benefits. If you do not have any room in the budget, consider enlisting the help of faculty from community colleges or other nonprofit groups that serve as conveners for other issues in this community engagement area. The tasks assigned to this role are consistently found in the nonprofit, health, and school sectors. However, we advocate hiring a community engagement liaison to address community immersion and collaboration at the C-suite level. The role should have the authority to make strategic decisions and have knowledge of the current state of the organization.

The Future of Work: A Subject Matter Expert Perspective

As we contemplate the future of work, practitioners need to address the critical questions of who, what, when, where, how, and why. By providing answers to these inquiries within the context of the future, we can fundamentally transform the preparation and development of the workforce during post-normal times. Organizations and industries that can strategically reimagine the future will be better positioned to sustain operations and compete effectively in global markets.

In examining the essential questions of who, what, when, where, how, and why, the creation of future scenarios can offer a range of perspectives on possible developments. By contemplating the shifts in political, economic, social, and technological landscapes, these scenarios serve not only as a tool for understanding potential outcomes but also as a strategic resource for businesses and industries. Such insights empower organizations to take a proactive stance in preparing and shaping the workforce of the future, ensuring they remain adaptable and competitive in an evolving environment. In today's complex and uncertain world, assuming past solutions will work for future problems is no longer feasible or sustainable.

Who

Once scenarios are developed, businesses should have a clearer understanding of the type of worker who will be impacted and how HR practices can be structured to recruit and train the necessary workers. At this stage, businesses and industries should explore the role of government and how policy will shape their HR practices. This step is critically important as the workforce landscape navigates post-normal times, where what was once known is no longer, as changing dynamics shape the governance at all levels. Understanding the "who" clarifies the stakeholders that will shape or be affected by future apprenticeship models. Demographic shifts, evolving worker expectations, and increasing diversity in the labor force require organizations to consider who is entering the talent pipeline and who is missing from it. By identifying future participants (apprentices, mentors, employers, educators, and community partners) organizations can design systems that are more inclusive, better aligned with workforce needs, and capable of responding to long-term labor market realities.

What

Understanding the "what" establishes the competencies, structures, and program components that may need to evolve. The technical skills required in high-demand industries are changing rapidly, and organizations must determine what knowledge, abilities, and support future workers will need to succeed. Clarifying "what" ensures that apprenticeship models remain relevant, industry-responsive, and grounded in the actual demands of future occupations, rather than outdated assumptions or legacy practices. Anticipating the types of jobs that may be affected by artificial intelligence, technological advancements, and political developments can enable businesses to adapt and cultivate a sustainable competitive advantage in the marketplace. This awareness directly influences workforce composition and size, as well as shaping human resource responses to shifting dynamics caused by the aforementioned developments.

When and Where

Understanding the "when" highlights the timing of changes and the urgency with which organizations must act. Labor shortages, accelerated retirements, and emerging technologies are reshaping industries faster than many systems can adapt. Considering "when" allows organizations to plan strategically, pace implementation, and avoid falling behind competitors who move more quickly to update their workforce strategies. Timing also matters for identifying when workers should be recruited, trained, upskilled, or transitioned into new roles. The traditional 9-to-5 workday and workplace location necessitate a deeper understanding of future trends. Businesses must adapt not only to when employees work but also to where they work.

Understanding the "where" describes the geographic, community, and contextual factors influencing apprenticeship design. Shifts in regional economies, population movement, remote or hybrid work models, and place-based labor needs all shape where apprenticeships should be offered and where partnerships should be cultivated. Recognizing "where" ensures that programs are responsive to local realities and positioned in the environments where talent is emerging and employers are growing. The rise of remote and hybrid work arrangements, spurred by the

COVID-19 pandemic in 2020, underscores this transition. As technology continues to advance, the factors of when and where will command even greater attention. Moreover, as employees increasingly seek a better work-life balance, HR policies must evolve to accommodate a generation of workers with these aspirations if organizations wish to attract and retain top talent.

How

Understanding the "how" details the operational processes and strategies that will be necessary to carry apprenticeship systems into the future. This includes how programs are structured, how learning occurs, how partnerships are built, and how success is measured. With industries becoming more complex and interconnected, the "how" becomes essential for ensuring that future apprenticeship models are scalable, efficient, and aligned with both worker needs and employer expectations. This phase of future planning represents where strategic intent translates into action. How will businesses and industries rise to meet the challenges evolving within the workplace? The path to answering this question is rooted in a clear understanding of the potential developments that lie ahead.

Why

Understanding the "why" serves to justify changes in HR policies and practices. Factors such as technological advancements and shifts in social and political circumstances will necessitate alterations in how businesses recruit, retain, and train the next generation of workers. Organizations that embrace this rationale will proactively address the demands of the future, whereas those who overlook the possibilities may find themselves merely reacting to changing dynamics, ultimately watching their competitive advantage wane in the marketplace.

Future-Oriented Thinking about Apprenticeships

When considering the future of apprenticeships, practitioners should explore how their current structure may evolve. Practitioners can initiate this exploration today by engaging in discussions that consider the state of apprenticeships from a long-term perspective, such as 50 years from now. Addressing the who, what, when, where, how, and why of apprenticeships will provide a foundational understanding upon which to build future-oriented or forward-thinking strategies that respond to the needs of both employer and apprentice.

Conclusion

Taken together, the recommendations in this chapter reinforce a central message: Sustainable talent expansion in technical industries requires coordinated action across policy, leadership, HR practice, and community partnership. The evolving landscape of the future of work demands leaders who understand both their identity and influence, HR systems that are adaptive and legally informed, and organizations that remain deeply connected to the communities they serve. As businesses confront shifting political, economic, and technological realities, adopting a proactive stance rather than a reactive posture will determine whether they thrive or fall behind. By embracing the guiding questions and strategic considerations outlined here, practitioners can better position their organizations to cultivate a resilient workforce, strengthen recruitment and retention across technical fields, and prepare for a future of work that is more complex, more interdependent, and filled with possibility.

Notes

1 Northouse, P. G. (2022). *Leadership: Theory and Practice*. Sage.
2 Komives, S., Longerbeam, S., Owen, J., Mainella, F., and Osteen, L. (2006). A Leadership Identity Development Model: Applications from a Grounded Theory. *Journal of College Student Development*, *47*, 401–418. 10.1353/csd.2006.0048.

Index

Note: Locators in *italic* indicate figures, in **bold** tables and in ***bold-italics*** boxes.

For Product Safety Concerns and Information please contact our EU representative GPSR@taylorandfrancis.com
Taylor & Francis Verlag GmbH, Kaufingerstraße 24, 80331 München, Germany

www.ingramcontent.com/pod-product-compliance
Ingram Content Group UK Ltd.
Pitfield, Milton Keynes, MK11 3LW, UK
UKHW022354190926
475702UK00015B/2282
9781032836362